MURDER
IN THE MISSIONS

A True Story

JEAN HARRINGTON

MERCIER PRESS

MERCIER PRESS
Cork
www.mercierpress.ie

© Jean Harrington, 2019

ISBN: 978 1 78117 712 9

Printed and bound in the EU.

For my children, Aoileann and Oisín,
who fill my days with endless wonder.

And for my mother, Aveen,
who epitomises kindness.

ACKNOWLEDGEMENTS

This book simply would not have been written without the help and advice of many people who knew Des and Rufus. I travelled to as many places that feature in the book as possible and interviewed Des and Rufus's friends, colleagues and families. Thank you to all who so generously gave their time.

In the Philippines, Fr Paul Glynn drew up a schedule for my trip and arranged countless meetings for me. It is safe to say this would be a far inferior book without his good-humoured assistance. For everything, Paul, you have my eternal gratitude.

Fr Yrap Nazareno kept me safe while travelling the dangerous roads around Mindanao and facilitated interviews with the Muslim friends of Des and Rufus at Mindanao State University. His insight into Rufus helped me better understand a man I had never met.

In Manila, Fr Brian Gore (who had been jailed by Marcos's regime) welcomed my family into the Columban house and was of great assistance in providing background information on Philippine society and politics. Thank you to Fr Kevin McHugh, who showed me around the beautiful Columban church in Malate, Manila, where he shared his memories of Des and Rufus.

Rufus's friends Sr Celia Eco and Venus Guibone sat with me for hours, sharing personal letters from Rufus, while detailing accounts of their lives together – I am very grateful to you both.

Thank you to Gerry Halley, Rufus's brother, who gave me access to personal letters, which allowed me to see a side to Rufus that only his family had previously experienced. Thank you also to John Halley, who carefully read the draft manuscript and contributed to the book.

The following people all contributed to the manuscript by generously sharing their stories: Lawan Minalang, Maguid Maruhom, Dr Moctar Matuan, Bai Connie Balindong, Noriah Elias, Fr Peter O'Neill, Fr Seán McDonagh, Fr Evergisto Bernaldez, Fr Nilo Tabania, Fr Michel de Gigord, Fr Michael Sinnott, Fr Dan O'Malley, Fr Rufil Quibranza and Bridget Hurley. John Robinson in the UK generously gave me access to his personal correspondence with Rufus.

The amount of research and raw material I gathered almost overwhelmed me at times. One person in particular, Fr Donie Hogan, kept me on track, always bringing me back to the manuscript. He has been my biggest advocate; the support he has offered over the years goes beyond words. He has been a mentor, friend and editor, carefully verifying facts, and passing the draft manuscript to the right person at the right time.

Thank you to the Tyrone Guthrie Centre in Annaghmakerrig, which gave me time and space to think and write, and to the people I met there. There truly is a creative community in Ireland with people who root for each other.

Thanks to all in Mercier Press, in particular to Noel O'Regan for asking all the right questions, and Commissioning Editor Patrick O'Donoghue.

In my private life there are people whose support give me strength in so many ways. My good friends Corina Bradley, Gillian Galvin, Orlagh Minnock, Caitríona Prestage, Áine Ní Chongaíle and Jackie Conlon. My late friend Catherine O'Reilly always supported my writing, attending festivals and events with me.

I am so lucky to have a large and supportive family, and I don't take it for granted. I owe everything to my mother, Aveen. Her love of reading and stories started me on my journey long ago, and her strength and resilience continue to inspire me.

Thank you to my late father, Robert, whose love and support still resonate throughout my life.

My sisters and brothers: Ann, Susie, Robert and Martin; you are my fabric and my world – mo cháirde, mo chlann, mo chroí!

During the time it took to research and write this book, my children, Aoileann and Oisín, gave me constant love, snuggles and distractions! I am so grateful for you!

For everyone who encouraged me to keep going with this book, I owe you my thanks. Every time someone asked how it was going, it spurred me on and gave me energy. Thanks to Siobhan Healy, Jane Hughes, Edward Fahy, Sally Coffee, Alan Faherty, Anthony Dunne, Geraldine and Colm Keaveny, and Suzanne Nelson.

Thanks to Ann Harrington, Aveen Harrington, Corina Bradley, Gillian Kavanagh, Orlagh Leonard, Patrick Kearns, Ric Panza and Craig Dinning, who all read parts of the manuscript at different stages and gave valuable feedback.

Finally, my thanks go to Des Hartford, Rufus Halley and their families.

To Des, I offer my gratitude for allowing me into his life, which must have been extraordinarily difficult as he reached the end of it. His foresight ensured I was accompanied by the right people until the manuscript was finished.

Although I never met Rufus Halley, I became acquainted with him through his family and many friends, as well as his personal letters and papers. His legacy lives on and the world is a little warmer because of him.

My hope is that this book will allow others to know Des and Rufus, and give an insight into the many people who are still working for peace in the Philippines.

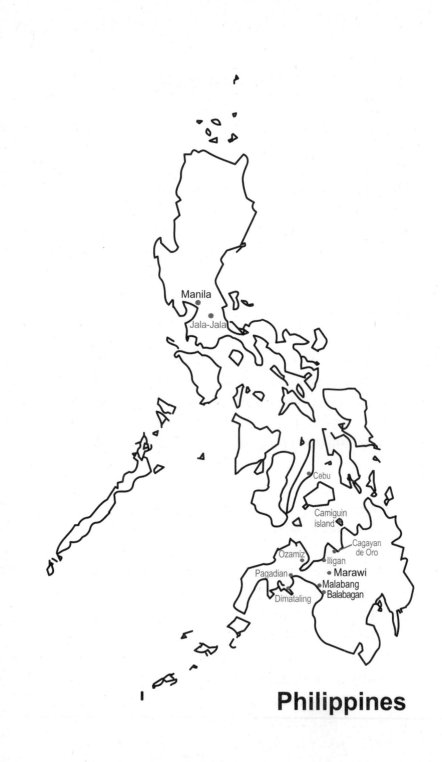

Philippines

INTRODUCTION

Many people ask why and how I got involved in Fr Des Hartford's and Fr Rufus Halley's stories. What would prompt someone who had no connection with the Catholic Church or the Philippines to start researching a complex tale of religion, politics and Muslim–Christian conflict, which spans four decades and crosses the world?

There is no simple answer to that question, except to say that I believed their stories needed to be told. In August 2001, I read an article in *The Irish Times* about an Irish priest who had been murdered while working in conflict resolution in the Philippines. The warmth of the murdered man, Fr Rufus Halley, was palpable from the way his friends and family members spoke about him. He knew he was living in a dangerous situation, and yet he remained there because he believed it was the right thing to do – that his actions of living peacefully would somehow influence his neighbours to lead a more peaceful life. This intrigued me.

The article went on to describe other Columban priests who were working in Muslim–Christian dialogue while living in the Philippines, and referenced how another Irish priest, Fr Des Hartford, had been kidnapped a few years previously. I was captivated by these men and wanted to know more. In late 2003, I rang the Missionary Society of St Columban in Navan and learned that Fr Des was now living there. To my surprise, I was put straight through to him, and I briefly outlined my idea about writing a book about his life. He was very polite but a little reserved about the concept. He said he would 'like some time to discern', so I promised to send him a letter with my proposal.

Some weeks later he contacted me and said he would be

happy for me to go ahead, and he would do whatever he could to give me access to everything I needed. There was a complication, however. He had advanced cancer at the time, and he knew he would not live to see the book completed. To this end, he introduced me to several of his friends and colleagues, knowing they would look after me when I travelled to the Philippines. I discovered a network of people who facilitated and supported my research, writing and editing. I spoke to as many as I could, and they all gave generously of their time and energy. Without the Columban Fathers, this book could not have happened. It is their story, as much as it is that of Des and Rufus.

It is also the story of the Philippines, a stunningly beautiful archipelago that has been devastated by corruption and greed since the Spanish invaded hundreds of years ago. The story of the conflict and violence is told through a narrative that wraps around these men's lives. It recreates the events and dialogue from interviews, diaries, letters and testimony.

***

Situated in south-east Asia, the Republic of the Philippines, named after King Philip II of Spain, is comprised of over 7,100 beautiful and exotic islands. The waters that surround it are all branches of the Pacific Ocean: the South China Sea lies to the west, the Sulu Sea and Celebes Sea are in the south and the Philippine Sea lies to the east. Approximately 105 million people live there, with 53 million living on the largest island, Luzon, which holds the capital city of Manila. Much of this book is based on the island of Mindanao, the second largest island in the archipelago, with a population of approximately 20 million people. There are eight major languages and almost one hundred dialects across the region.

Behind the outstanding beauty of the country lies a troubled history. Being under colonial rule for almost 400 years has left a mark on the Filipinos and their culture. First the Spanish and then the Americans invaded.

Spanish explorers arrived in the archipelago in the sixteenth century and, under Spanish rule, they attempted to convert the inhabitants to Christianity. Islam was already an established religion in the archipelago at the time, having first arrived around the fourteenth century via Arab migrants and traders. The Spanish halted the further spread of Islam in the central and northern regions by driving existing Muslims out of those areas and forcibly converting those who remained. The most notable legacy of the Spanish colonisers, and one which still causes ripples today, was the Christianisation of the Philippines. Approximately ninety-two per cent of the current population is Christian – predominantly Roman Catholic – while Muslims represent less than five per cent of the remaining population.

The Spanish failed to conquer the Muslim strongholds of Mindanao and Sulu in the south, where the people had strong pride in their cultural heritage and fought to maintain their independence. The Spanish named these Filipino Muslims 'Moros' after the Moors of northern Africa. The treatment of the Muslims at the hands of the Spanish led to centuries of tension and mistrust between Muslims and Christians, with many Muslims coming to resent the general population of Christians for their treatment.

A revolution against the Spanish colonisers from 1896 to 1898 ended Spanish rule, but this outcome coincided with the Spanish–American war in 1898.[1] The result of this war was the Treaty of Paris, signed on 10 December 1898, which ceded the Philippines to the United States.[2]

Filipino nationalists did not want to move from one coloniser to another and, led by Emilio Aguinaldo, sought their independence from the United States. Another revolution and open warfare broke out in February 1899.[3] The US tried to brutally suppress this movement, and the war continued for three years. Approximately 200,000 people died from violence, famine and disease.

Despite this intense resistance from the Filipinos, with the Cooper Act of 1902 the Philippines became an American colony. The Americans took over the country with gusto. Not content with merely settling on the largest island, they encouraged their people to move and take over the native lands.

Governor Leonard Wood espoused the resources of the island of Mindanao in particular. 'It is difficult to get a more beautiful place than Mindanao,' he said. 'People should plod to this island, just as they did to the wild American west. Their example will inspire and their work will educate the locals.'[4]

Prior to the American invasion, no one had personal title to the land they were using in Mindanao. The use of land was under the stewardship of the *datu*, the leader of the community. However, at this point in time, the *datus* sold the land to the foreign Christians, selling out their own people.

Over the next two decades, the American attitude towards the Philippines' desire for independence gradually changed and the United States passed several pieces of legislation towards returning the country to its people. In 1934, the Philippine Independence Act, also known as the Tydings-McDuffie Act, provided for an independent Philippines, subject to a ten-year transition period. In 1935, the transitional government approved a constitution, which included a political system that was almost identical to that of the United States in its structure. This limited the elected president to a six-year term, without the opportunity to run for re-election.[5] In 1940, the 1935 constitution was amended by the National Assembly of the Philippines. This changed the term limit of the president to four years, with the possibility of being re-elected for a second term.[6]

The drive towards independence was halted between 1941 and 1945, because the Japanese invaded and occupied the Philippines during this period. When the Japanese were eventually expelled, plans for independence resumed. On 4 July 1946, after nearly 400 years of bloodshed and battle, the Philippines became an independent nation.

For the Muslims in the southern Philippines, however, being governed by Filipino Christians was even less agreeable than living under foreign rule. The new government encouraged Christians in the northern and central regions to move to the south, where the land was more fertile and less densely populated. As a result, the Muslims became a minority in their own homeland.

The memories of former injustices burned deep in the minds of the people who were displaced during this period, and at the same time the Muslim and Christian communities found themselves in competition for land and resources. Not long after the Filipinos had fought for freedom from colonial rule, they took up arms against one another, particularly on the island of Mindanao.

I

DIALOGUE AMID RISING TENSIONS

CHAPTER 1

A life unlike your own can be your teacher.

St Columban

It was April 1973 and the island of Mindanao in the south of the Philippines was descending into a war between the Muslim population and their Christian neighbours. No one was safe, not even the priests who worked in the locality. Fr Peter O'Neill from Co. Tyrone had taken to sleeping between sandbags on the floor, as he feared an attack from the Muslim rebels who were targeting Christians in Dimataling.

One night, gunshots blazed through his bedroom window on the second floor of his two-storey residence, which was located between the church and the school. He lay there, terrified, quietly trying to still his breathing until they had gone, and thanking God for his foresight with the sandbags.

As soon as he was sure the gunmen were gone, Peter ran downstairs to check on the two schoolboys who were staying there. He found them alive, thankfully, but traumatised. Quickly, they prepared to leave, gathering water, supplies and as many of their belongings as they could carry. After all, the gunmen could come back at any moment.

In the dead of night, they fled towards Colojo, a small village in the hills that was a trek of an hour and a half from Dimataling. Colojo felt like the safe option, as it was the boys' home and was populated only by Christians. There were no proper cement or tarmac roads out of Dimataling, a remote town on the large island, so they trekked instead along dirt tracks and even through jungle in places, in case they came across more trouble. They travelled quickly, refusing to take a break. Still, it was near dawn by the time they reached the village.

Peter spent the next few weeks there in hiding. As the violence intensified, he began to send a constant stream of refugees away from the mountains of Mindanao. And there was only one place he could think of to send them: to his friend and colleague from the Missionary Society of St Columban, Fr Des Hartford, who resided in Pagadian city, a three-hour boat trip away. Des would help them, Peter was certain.

**

Although he had not personally witnessed the terror the villagers were fleeing, Des Hartford, from the small town of Lusk in north Co. Dublin, knew what had driven the evacuees to abandon their homes in the mountain villages and seek sanctuary. The tension in the air was palpable.

One day a young woman arrived with her three children. Distraught and overwhelmed by unimaginable grief, she broke down while trying to speak about the horrors she had witnessed. Her husband, she said, had been shot dead. Her home was burned to the ground and she'd lost everything.

Perhaps for the first time in his ministry, Des, a tall, quiet Irishman, could not think of any comforting words to say, so he just listened.

The members of the Missionary Society of St Columban were among the few to bear witness to the murderous carnage which, at times, threatened to engulf the entire island of Mindanao but remained largely unknown to the outside world.

In the days that followed the initial attacks, Des listened to more villagers recount stories of how Muslim gunmen had murdered, tortured and maimed Christians in cold blood. To Des, the deaths represented the demise of the last vestiges of trust and charity among the island's different cultures, which had slowly eroded over the past few decades.

While the killings terrified Des, he was more frightened by the utter hatred and mistrust that such murders caused. This was best illustrated by the language each side used to describe the other. The Muslim bandits were referred to as *barracuda*, 'the fighting fish', by the Christians, while the Muslims called the Christians who took up arms against them the *ilaga*, a derogatory word that means 'rats'.

Des didn't believe hatred alone was the cause. He was a rational person who knew there was always an underlying motive for the violence. The killings weren't truly sectarian in nature; their cause was more complicated than that. The roots of the murderous terror that threatened to engulf the island, he felt, lay in the political corruption that infiltrated almost every facet of society in the Philippine archipelago.

On 21 September 1972, months before this spate of killings began, President Ferdinand Marcos issued Proclamation 1081, which imposed martial law on the whole country and also closed the Philippine Congress.[1] It had a catastrophic effect on democracy. Journalists, student leaders and trade union activists were arrested, along with those who opposed the president. A further effect of Proclamation 1081 was to shut down newspapers and bring the mass media under the control of the president.

Marcos put the military in charge and gave them permission to do whatever was necessary to keep him and his cronies safe. Seventy thousand people who had connections with the workers' movement and tenants' rights were arrested and imprisoned. Marcos's circle of supporters took trading companies and government agencies for themselves. The country's wealth was going to a small selection of powerful people, who sent the money offshore to foreign banks, all the while overseen and protected by the military.[2]

Like other dictators, Marcos defended his decision to effectively abolish democracy by claiming to be protecting it. He said martial law was necessary to counteract the threat posed by the New People's Army (NPA), a communist-inspired group, and the Moro National Liberation Front (MNLF), a paramilitary organisation dedicated to the creation of an independent Muslim state in Mindanao.

The MNLF was formed in 1971 by Nur Misuari, whose radical interpretation of Islam and proclamations against the Marcos regime attracted a groundswell of support among the island's Muslim population. It was a disciplined organisation that had a profound influence on other rebel groups because of the tight way it was run.[3] Misuari wanted all Muslim insurgents to unite and align under the MNLF umbrella. Many insurgent groups did join the MNLF because they were allowed to maintain their individual identity while joining with the larger, more disciplined organisation. Others remained outside the MNLF, but they too were taking up arms against the government's troops.

The number of armed insurgents in 1973 was estimated at between 15,000 and 30,000.[4] While their fight was with the government, it was the ordinary citizens of the Philippines who suffered the most in this protracted conflict. By the end of the century, more than 100,000 had been killed by the violence.

The motivation behind Marcos's decision to suspend democracy was not, as everyone knew, to protect the Philippines against a Muslim insurgency; the order was aimed at ensuring that Marcos could retain absolute power. The Philippine constitution limited the presidential reign to no more than eight consecutive years in office. Having held the presidency already for eight years, Marcos was out of time. Martial law allowed him to suspend the constitution and gave him the extension of power he so badly desired.

There were many societal changes under Marcos's rule. From 1975 to 1983, the country's debt increased threefold and the local currency, the peso, lost half its value. The government had borrowed money from international banks, allegedly to build dams, motorways and factories, but many of these projects never materialised. The money disappeared into the president's pockets.[5]

The size of the military also increased hugely during this time, and high-ranking officers became rich and powerful. They attacked the Catholic Church, especially the clergy and lay people who spoke out against them. Soldiers defended land barons and logging and mining companies, and removed people from their lands with little or no compensation. They imprisoned people without trial. They used local people to go into the mountains to negotiate with the NPA, and if a villager refused to help, they burned down every house in the village. They covered their tracks by saying the villagers were part of the NPA.

In response to Proclamation 1081, the MNLF launched what was to become a fully fledged armed insurgency in Mindanao. They first focused on the city of Marawi, the inhabitants of which were almost all of Muslim faith and culture. After Marawi, the fighting quickly spread, and the MNLF campaign soon descended into an overwhelming assault, particularly in rural areas. The insurgents murdered those of other faiths and cultures whom they had lived alongside in peace for generations, possibly because the military was viewed as Christian.

Des, along with his fellow Columbans, watched in horror at the slaughter that ensued.

***

The Missionary Society of St Columban's relationship with the archipelago began in 1929 when, at the request of the Archbishop of Manila, it sent two priests, Patrick Kelly and Michael Cuddigan, to serve in the parish of Malate, in Manila.[6]

The Philippines was not 'in the missions' as outlined by Roman Catholic canon law, because approximately ninety per cent of its inhabitants were recorded as being Roman Catholic. It was seen as an unusual choice for the Columbans, who were intended to do 'apostolic work among infidel peoples'.[7] So going to a country where, on paper, the vast majority of people were Roman Catholics was not an obvious choice. The truth was, however, that hundreds of parishes had been abandoned and some had been left vacant since the Spanish ceded the Philippines to the United States of America in 1898 as part of the Treaty of Paris.[8] The Archbishop of Manila, Michael O'Doherty, needed priests and had pleaded with the Columban superior general, Michael O'Dwyer, to send help.

About a quarter of Roman Catholics in the country at this time had left the Roman Catholic Church to join the Philippine Independent Church, presided over by Gregorio Aglipay, who had led a campaign to free the church from Spanish dominance.[9] Many saw very little difference between the two churches. However, the Columban priests were disheartened when they saw that former Roman Catholics were content to burn candles before statues and seemed to know nothing about the Eucharist.[10]

The missionaries had their work cut out for them. Over the next few years, more and more Irish missionaries arrived and began to care for the spiritual needs of the Roman Catholic inhabitants of the islands. The Columban mission, as the missionaries saw it, was to rekindle the faith of the people, rebuild churches and train catechists.

This work ground to a halt for a period during the Second World War, when the Japanese invaded the archipelago. The Columbans suffered greatly during the war and many were forced to leave the country.

For those who were able to stay, many suffered deprivation, living in the mountains where they were protected, fed and sheltered by friendly Catholics. Others were tortured and killed, however. One Columban, Francis Douglas from New Zealand, was hauled away in the middle of the night on 27 July 1943. He was never seen again and, even today, the Columbans are still trying to learn of his fate and the details of his presumed martyrdom.

The missionary work of the Columbans began again once the invaders were defeated and had left the Philippines. Their mission was successful because the Columbans placed great emphasis on training lay people to work in their own local parishes. Missionary zeal for the spiritual upliftment of the parishioners was not the only purpose of the Columban missionaries, though. The Columbans were also social advocates, whose religious beliefs were grounded in the struggle for social justice.

It was this underlying aspect of the Columbans' work that Des Hartford was passionate about. By the time he arrived in the archipelago in 1968, the Columbans had developed an advanced theological approach to their mission. They recognised that the poverty they encountered in the Philippines was structurally related to decisions and behaviour not only in the Philippines, but also in other parts of the world.

Des came to realise, like the other priests of his generation, that attempting to strengthen the people's spiritual life alone was not sufficient. The Columbans had to support their congregation in all their needs. He and his colleagues believed the injustices and poverty their parishioners were experiencing could not be ignored. They became a part of their communities and took action to help their parishioners in all areas of their lives. When he was a young boy in Ireland dreaming of joining the missions, however, he had no idea how complex his life would become as a priest.

CHAPTER 2

If you want to make peace with your enemy, you have to work with your enemy. Then he becomes your partner.

Nelson Mandela

Desmond Hartford was the youngest of four children and experienced a sheltered, rural upbringing in a farming community in north Co. Dublin. Even as a young boy he was drawn to the priesthood. His family had *The Far East* magazine delivered to their home and he read the articles sent from the missions with fervour, memorising the details from the countries in which the Columbans were based.

He first met a missionary priest when Fr Aidan McGrath visited his school, De La Salle College in Skerries, in the 1950s. The priest recounted how he had been imprisoned in China while working on the missions. The element of danger did not dissuade the young boy from Dublin. In fact, this story attracted him more. He wanted to spread his faith and share it with people who didn't believe. It was the visit of another Columban priest, however, during his final year of school that cemented his decision to become a missionary priest.

Des had been contemplating the priesthood for some time, but hearing Fr Michael Balfe speak so passionately to a room full of schoolboys about life in the missions confirmed for him that joining the Missionary Society of St Columban would be the right move. In September 1961, when he was eighteen, Des enrolled in the seminary in Dalgan Park, Co. Meath, along with forty-four other students. Seven years later, he was one of nineteen seminarians ordained to the priesthood.

In September 1968, after his ordination, he was sent to the Columban headquarters in Ozamiz on the island of Mindanao in the Philippines, where he spent seven months studying the local language, Cebuano/Visayan. Language often distinguishes the Philippines' Christian and Muslim populations from one another. The one Des studied is known as Cebuano because it is spoken on the island of Cebu. It is one of a group of sister languages known as Visayan, spoken in the central islands of the Philippines. The Christians in Mindanao also use Cebuano, however, because most of the settlers who migrated to Mindanao after the Second World War came from the province of Cebu. The Muslim population in the island's Lanao province, on the other hand, speak Maranao, the language that was spoken in some parts of Mindanao for centuries before the arrival of the Cebuano settlers.

It was vital that Des could communicate in the language of his parishioners, but he struggled with it. He didn't have a natural facility for languages and Cebuano had a totally different structure to the Irish and French he had learned in school. He persevered with it, however, and made time each day to study the grammar, structure and vocabulary. He also immersed himself in the local community, practising speaking as often as possible.

At the end of seven months, his official language training was complete and he was beginning to feel comfortable enough to hold a conversation in Cebuano. After leaving language school, Des was assigned to a small parish on Camiguin island, situated in the Bohol Sea, just to the north of Mindanao. The volcanic island has hot and cold springs, white sandy beaches and rich jungles. It was a peaceful place for the young priest to acclimatise to working in a ministry.

Fr Martin Ryan, the parish priest, initiated him into the local pastoral scene. As well as looking after the spiritual needs of his parishioners, Martin actively helped defend the rights of the poorest in the congregation. Many priests in the Philippines were becoming active during this period, as the establishment of the Second Vatican Council in 1965 had seen the beginning of noteworthy church involvement in social issues.

Martin was working with an organisation called the Federation of Free Farmers, set up in 1953 by laymen who had been trained by the Jesuits.[1] Most local farmers on the island didn't own the land they farmed; they were merely tenants. Under the 1954 Agricultural Tenancy Act of the Philippines, all rice crops were to be shared out fifty-fifty between the tenant farmers and the landowner. According to the Act, expenses should be deducted before the money was shared, but most of the wealthy landowners took the expenses out of their tenant farmers' share. The tenant farmers, supported by the Federation of Free Farmers, stood up against the landowners and insisted the profit was divided according to the law.

Many of the wealthy landowners in the area were prominent in the church and they were very unhappy with the priests supporting the tenant farmers. This caused conflict in the parish, and it was the first time Des experienced tensions between the rich and the poor. He and Martin attended meetings with the Federation of Free Farmers, and listened night after night, horrified by how the poorest in the land had their rights trampled on, without any support from official sources. Des was quickly learning that in the Philippines, religion, politics and war were irrevocably intertwined.

***

The eruption of sectarian violence among the people of Mindanao in the early 1970s had a catastrophic effect on the Roman Catholic Church in the Philippines. In October 1970,

Fr Martin Dempsey, a Columban priest, was shot dead in Balabagan, Lanao del Sur, by two of his students because he reprimanded one of them.

Des travelled to the funeral in Balabagan on a bus. It was his first time travelling through predominately Muslim areas and he felt very uncomfortable. The bus stopped on the way, allowing the occupants to refresh themselves and get some snacks. An elderly Muslim lady was selling peanuts at a stand on the side of the road, and Des approached her to buy some. As a tall, thin, white man, he stood out immediately among the locals. The peanuts cost just two pesos, but he had only a fifty-peso bill on him at the time. He instinctively didn't trust her simply because she was a Muslim, so he said, 'You go and get me the change first, and then I'll give you the fifty pesos.' She willingly obliged him.

When he was back on the bus, Des reflected on what had happened. *Where did I get this mistrust? Why did I not trust that old Muslim lady? Did I think she was going to run off with my fifty pesos?* He realised that while ministering to the population of his parishes, which were 100 per cent Christian, he'd picked up some of the prejudices the Christians held against the Muslims. He resolved to never again let other people's prejudices affect his own thought process.

The Catholic Church continued to monitor the tensions between the Muslim and Christian populations in Mindanao. The church leaders watched it fester and could see the conflict develop and worsen.

There were so many violent incidents. For example, in June 1971, in the predominantly Muslim town of Manili in Cotabato, armed men who were dressed in the uniform of the army went into the local mosque and opened fire, killing about sixty-five men, women and children.[2] The fact that the killings happened in a holy place added to the sense of outrage in the town. In *Revolt in Mindanao*, T. J. S. George says the outstanding feature of the massacre was that it was essentially meaningless[3] – though it was later suggested that it was an act of revenge for the killing of Christians in the area. Following this massacre, thousands of Muslims evacuated to the Lake Lanao area around Marawi. Christians were also attacked in response, and many had their houses burned down.

Until that point the Catholic Church had strategically avoided getting involved in the conflict out of fear that such a move could be misinterpreted. Its decision to finally intervene in the problem was brought about by the work of a diocesan bishop from Cebu called Bienvenido Tudtud. In 1971, he became the bishop of the prelature of Iligan, a city on the island of Mindanao in the province of Lanao del Norte.[4]

Bishop 'Benny' Tudtud, perhaps more than anyone else, found himself consumed by the effects of the conflict. He was an educated man who had well-informed opinions on the political corruption and sectarianism that had forced its way into his ministry. He recognised that the violence, which simmered below the surface of everyday life, would inevitably resurface again and again unless the two faiths engaged in dialogue. The prejudices between the communities were so deeply rooted that children in his Christian community of Cebu learned phrases like 'Never turn your back on a Muslim', or 'The only good Muslim is a dead Muslim.' Of his upbringing, he said he was chastised as a child with 'You are a wicked Moro', while his eighty-five-year-old father was 'nostalgic for the days when Muslims weren't allowed upstairs'.[5]

Three years into his role as bishop, Tudtud came to the realisation that the Christian leaders needed to learn about Islam so they would be able to engage in meaningful dialogue with Muslims. It would assist them in better understanding the religious convictions of their Muslim neighbours, and the Muslims would be appreciative of the Christians' interest in their religion.

To start the process, Tudtud decided he must first study Islam at the Pontifical Institute for Arabic and Islamic Studies in Rome, Italy. He undertook Islamology from October 1974 to June 1975. While there, Tudtud developed a direct line of communication with Pope Paul VI, who wanted to learn more about the Muslim–Christian conflict in Mindanao.[6] In private meetings held with the pontiff, Tudtud outlined the growing problem. The pope understood the complexity of the situation and encouraged Tudtud to pursue whatever course of action he thought necessary. Tudtud would later write that the Holy Father concluded reconciliation was needed. 'The Gospel demands that we rise up – not only above our unfounded prejudices, but specially that we should rise above our well-founded prejudices.'[7]

The two men agreed that creating a dialogue between the two communities was one of the most pressing needs at the time. To create a dialogue that would last and endure through all the difficulties of the conflict would, however, demand a serious study of Islam. Tudtud knew that dialogue was a real challenge for the people he was assigned to serve, especially since most of the prejudices in the region stemmed from the pain of prolonged violent encounters between them. This deep-rooted history of conflict and killings made it difficult for each side to see the other in an unbiased way.[8]

Pope Paul VI proposed that Tudtud create a special ecclesiastical jurisdiction that would be dedicated to the dialogue between the Christians and Muslims of Mindanao. The creation of a prelature, a religious office to carry out specific pastoral duties and missions, would demonstrate the Catholic Church's commitment to solving the complicated problem. This was a challenge that would consume Tudtud for the rest of his life.

In 1975, Tudtud returned to the city of Iligan but quickly realised he could not adequately respond to the challenge without neglecting the pastoral needs of the Christians. In October 1976, he proposed to the pope that they divide up the diocese of Iligan and turn the city of Marawi and surrounding areas into a separate prelature. Because Pope Paul VI was supporting the project, which was considered radical for its time, Tudtud was pushing an open door. On 8 December 1976, the prelature of St Mary's in Marawi was established, with Tudtud presiding over it as bishop.

The prelature was quite different from the original concept that had been conceived in Rome; it became a geographical jurisdiction that focused on the needs of the people of Marawi, who were predominately Muslim. The Christians in the area represented different denominations. The new prelature also reached outside the city of Marawi into a few areas in Lanao del Norte, as well as the whole of the province of Lanao del Sur – two regions that were mostly inhabited by people of the Muslim faith.

Tudtud conceived three complementary dimensions to the prelature, each one equally as important as the next. The first was the contemplative side, which emphasised the importance of prayer. This meant that the dialogue must be rooted in prayer and in quiet contemplation. He believed he must know himself and his faith intimately before he could think about engaging meaningfully with others of different faiths.

The second dimension was one of dialogue. Tudtud recognised that, to begin dialogue and to be able to converse with people of the Muslim faith, it was important to have a good knowledge of Islam; it also meant that all Christians should be respectful of the religion. The word 'dialogue' presupposed that one culture respected the other; after all, those in Mindanao who would initiate dialogue had to realise they were in dialogue because of the conflict that already existed, one aggravated by deep prejudices on both sides. Those who entered into dialogue had to be ready to face the possibility of humiliation or, as Tudtud said, the dialogue would be a farce.[9]

The third dimension of the prelature was what he described as immersion. To Tudtud this meant to immerse oneself in Islam while remaining faithful to Christianity. This dimension is simply to live with and be with Muslims. It is not an attempt to 'do' anything other than live peacefully alongside Muslim neighbours, respecting their values and culture.

Tudtud's beliefs were grounded in realism. For dialogue to be successful, he knew that certain conditions had to prevail. Aside from the niceties of religious dialogue, he knew that both sides needed to be prepared to grow and change their own mindsets to foster peace; he also knew that any discussions had to be two-sided and that each side, be it Muslim or Christian, had to enter the discussion with honesty and sincerity. Most importantly, they had to see themselves as equals.

According to Tudtud, the Christians had to approach the life of dialogue with a freshness that would defy their prejudices: 'We are preparing the Christians to absorb the particular spirituality of dialogue. And so our main objective would be to form a community of Christians able to offer this attitude of dialogue to their Muslim brothers and sisters … I'd like to see here in Marawi a Christian community that is aware of a new way of expressing its faith.'[10]

Tudtud started looking for volunteer priests to join his new prelature and community. For a handful of the Columban priests who lived among the poor of Mindanao, the creation of Tudtud's prelature was a godsend. The objectives of its mission lent itself to their philosophy, which was rooted in social justice. The Missionary Society of St Columban committed itself and its resources to the project. In many ways, it became the priority of the priests involved, although at any particular time there were only about six Columban priests actively working in the prelature.

***

Not every Columban priest was enthused by the creation of the new prelature, however. Fr Des Hartford's first reaction to it was to avoid it at all costs. Des knew very little about Islamic history and he had no desire to learn more, even though he was alert to the political tensions and undercurrents in Mindanao. He saw his mission as one that was to look after the needs of the Christians in the Philippines.

'I knew they were looking for volunteers to enter into the Muslim–Christian dialogue, but I had absolutely no attraction to it. I didn't know anything about Muslims and I didn't want to. I was very happy with what I was doing with the Christians and I'd absolutely no interest or desire to get into this Muslim–Christian dialogue.'[11]

By the time the prelature was established in 1976, Des had been based in Pagadian for about four years and had become the parish priest. The extreme violence he witnessed a few years earlier had quietened down a little. Negotiations had taken place between the Philippine government and the MNLF, which resulted in the signing of a peace agreement in Tripoli in Libya that year. In return for autonomy in the southern provinces of Mindanao, the MNLF agreed to a ceasefire.

After the signing of the peace agreement, life began to return to normal for the people of Pagadian and for the Columbans. Still, tensions simmered between the two faiths, although they were almost imperceptible at times.

Fr Peter O'Neill never did return to his parochial house in Dimataling following his miraculous escape the night he was attacked in 1973. Having sent scores of refugees to Des in Pagadian city, he himself was now reassigned to Pagadian, where he lived with Des. By the time he arrived there, the sectarian violence in the area had largely subsided. Peter believed he no longer needed to sleep with one eye open.

But tragedy was never far away in the archipelago. In August 1976, a massive earthquake erupted in the sea beside Pagadian. Des woke up in the middle of the night to noise and vibrations so strong he couldn't sit up in bed. In the aftermath, he discovered that the earthquake had destroyed only a small number of houses in the city; most of the destruction was caused by the tsunami that came afterwards.

Within five minutes of the earthquake occurring, waves of about nine metres high struck the shore, wiping out entire families whose houses were built on stilts on the shoreline. The Columbans were lucky as their house was elevated about 150 metres inland and the water didn't reach as far as the house. The tide destroyed everything in its path. Thousands of people drowned during that disaster, many of whom were children. Some of the bodies were never found.

The Columbans spent the next few months dealing with the fallout of the human tragedy: helping displaced families, counselling, arranging funeral Masses, and simply sitting and listening to the stories from the community.

'Quite a number of those killed were Muslims, and we often had meetings with Muslims and Christians together after the earthquake. I was always amazed by the faith of the Muslims.

They always used to see it from a perspective of faith. This was my first introduction to their faith,' Des said.[12]

Des went home to Ireland for a holiday in 1977 and, while there, attended a retreat in the Manresa Jesuit Retreat House in Dollymount. This would prove to be a defining moment in his life, although at the time he had no idea how.

Part of the retreat involved thirty days of silence to allow the participants to concentrate on prayer. Des was permitted to speak only to his appointed director during an agreed time each day. The director was a priest who offered guidance to Des with his prayer, if assistance was required.

Self-imposed silence wasn't Des's type of religion, but it did give him the opportunity to clear his mind. It was during this retreat that he realised he needed to decide what he'd do when he returned to the Philippines.

He told his course director he wanted to continue working within the Christian community, but he was not sure in what role. The course director, sensing Des's internal confusion, told him to write down all the possibilities that were available to him, and to pray for guidance. Des did as instructed, but nothing seemed to happen. Another two days passed and Des indicated that he was still confused. The director asked if he had explored all his options. Des, who always believed in honesty regardless of the outcome, replied, 'There are options that are not on the list, but I'm not going to do them. I'm not interested and I'm not going to do them.'

'Put them on the list. You have to.'

'The inclusion of these would be a pointless exercise.'

'Put them on the list!'

The Columbans were working with the poor in Pakistan at that time, so Des reluctantly added Pakistan and Marawi to his list of possibilities.

He spent the next few days in intense prayer and contemplation, trusting in God that he would be guided towards the right
decision. Towards the end of the retreat, Des experienced what
he described as an encounter with Christ.

This incident happened when he was sitting in a small room
that looked out onto a compact garden. He was praying without
being too focused or concentrating on anything in particular,
when suddenly he got a very strong sense that Christ was sitting
in the chair beside him, wearing Muslim clothing unique to
Marawi. Des jumped out of his chair and said, 'Forget about
that!' and left the room.

He tried to put the bizarre image out of his mind, but it kept
invading his thoughts every time he attempted to pray. Finally
he surrendered and let the image in. He decided to try to get
into a dialogue with the Lord about it. He spent five more days
praying. On the last day of the retreat, the message was clear and
unequivocal.

'Okay, Lord! I'll go to Marawi,' he said resignedly.

CHAPTER 3

My apostolate must be the apostolate of goodness.
In seeing me, people should say to one another:
'Since this man is so good, his religion must be good.'

Charles de Foucauld, 1909

Fr Des returned to the Philippine archipelago in early 1978 and joined the prelature of St Mary's in Marawi, where he was assigned to work in a town called Karomatan (now known as Sultan Naga Dimaporo). There was a handful of Columban priests already working on the prelature project and, by the time he arrived, the work was well underway. The bishop had come to describe the project as 'the dialogue of life', which endorsed the principle of a more peaceful co-existence.

In accordance with long-standing Catholic traditions, Bishop Tudtud had drafted several ecclesiastical statements on behalf of the prelature, outlining his vision. These served as a focal point for Des and his colleagues, and were vital in keeping them focused on the direction they were moving in, given the history of prejudice between Muslims and Christians in that part of Mindanao.

Tudtud told Des that it was only through living with Muslims and learning about their world that he would be able to engage in open dialogue with them. This was a precondition of the dialogue, which the bishop referred to as kenosis, or displacement: 'putting aside some of my own thought and behaviour patterns in order to make a place for those of a brother'.[1]

Des immersed himself in the vision while working in the parish of Karomatan. One of his virtues was his ability to take instruction and expose himself to new ideas, even if he didn't fully understand them. Soon he realised that he wanted to experience kenosis personally. Therefore, in the summer of 1978, he asked Tudtud to appoint another priest to take his place in his parish, which would enable him to live in a Muslim community. This experience would also provide him with an opportunity to learn Maranao, the language spoken by the Muslims in that part of Mindanao. He was already fluent in Cebuano, but to dialogue with the Muslims he needed to speak their language fluently.

This plan was a radical one for the Columban priest. Would he be accepted? Would he be treated with suspicion? For the first time in his adult life, Des knew he would be a complete outsider. He wouldn't have a particular role in the community in which he lived. Part of him was exhilarated at the prospect, as he believed it would force him to discover what it meant to be a true missionary. The Christian Filipinos had always related to him as a priest; now he was going into a situation where he would merely be a man. He was undeterred, however, and put his trust in God. But in practice he didn't know where to begin or where it would end.

The opportunity to live among Muslims presented itself through Luna Noran, an acquaintance of Des who worked with an NGO on the island. When Luna heard that Des wanted to live among the Muslim community, he recommended that he contact a friend of his, Sultan Lawan Minalang, who was living in a *barrio* called Bauyan.[2] In the Philippines, sultans are traditionally religious and political leaders in communities. People respect their sultans and go to them for advice on both practical and spiritual matters.

Des met Lawan and explained how he wanted to immerse himself in a Muslim community. Des was clear in what he wanted to do, but he needed help in achieving his goal. The introduction was fortuitous, as Lawan and his wife, Apao, invited the priest to live with them in their home, which was a small wooden and brick dwelling protected from the elements by a galvanised roof.

Des was at first surprised by the offer, but later he realised he had anticipated some act of generosity, as he believed the journey was God's will and could not fail. He soon discovered the family was willing to give freely. He was even given his own bedroom at the expense of the numerous children, who had previously used the room. Six of them attended school in Cebu and stayed there during the school term, but the three youngest boys and a baby girl lived in the small house with their parents.

He moved in, expecting to find countless differences between them, but very quickly he saw how alike they were; their basic human needs were exactly like his, and this proved to be the basis for any dialogue. Des's presence in the *barrio* attracted a certain amount of curiosity in the neighbourhood. He was conscious of this from the moment of his arrival, although he was greeted only in a friendly manner by the locals.

The transition from priest to lay person took some time. He was focused on learning the language, culture and religion, but he had to do so in a context where he was not needed in the life of the community. Within this *barrio*, people weren't approaching him saying, 'You're needed for a baptism, you're needed for a wedding. There's a Mass here.' The fact that he no longer had an official role in the place he lived led him to think about his place in society. *What does it mean to be a Christian rather than a priest in a particular setting? How do I live as a Christian?* With the emphasis now on being a Christian rather than a priest, he found himself trying to relate to ordinary Muslims on ordinary matters.

He wasn't the only one who found the arrangement new and unusual, however. The people often questioned Lawan on why he allowed a Columban priest to live in his house. Rather than debate the intricacies of kenosis, Lawan formulated a simple response that satisfied the villagers' curious minds: Des wanted to learn their language.

The priest set a routine for himself, which he followed each day. He woke at 5 a.m. and went for a run. Upon his return to the house, he bathed himself using the *kabo*, a primitive shower system used by the family. This comprised a scoop and a bucket in the bathroom. When he finished, he pumped water at a nearby well and filled the big bucket for the other occupants of the house.

After his shower, he read his Bible, said some prayers and then had breakfast, which consisted of coffee and small bread rolls the locals called *pandesal*. After breakfast he would go to the market and talk to the villagers who were out shopping.

At noon each day he returned home and had lunch with the family before taking a siesta. The siesta was very important to Des, and he made sure to rest every day. It is an essential part of the lifestyle of those living in a hot tropical climate where the sun and the heat drain the energy of the people, especially the foreigners.

Des quickly blended into local life in the months following his arrival in Bauyan. He did all the predictable things, such as eating the local foods and learning the language, but it was his commitment to learning the ways of Islam that endeared him to the inhabitants of the *barrio*. He developed an affinity with the local people, and grew especially close to Lawan, to the point where the two men were able to joke about religion. Des learned that Lawan could be a master of jokes because of his irreverent sense of humour. On occasion, Lawan would ask Des if his bishop was really God.

There was a more serious side to his time there, however. He dedicated himself to spending time at the mosque in the *barrio*, often in Lawan's company. During the holy month of Ramadan, he steadfastly observed the fasting rule and didn't eat during the day. The practice, which was conceived by Bishop Tudtud as part of his expanding philosophy, was called *duyog Ramadan*, a Visayan term that means to 'go with' or 'accompany people in Ramadan'. Other Christians who were involved in this practice also didn't eat in front of their Muslim friends during Ramadan. *Duyog Ramadan* was aimed at encouraging the two religions to live in solidarity with each other.

Des adapted his practices to accommodate his hosts and their friends. He would visit a local priest in Karomatan every Friday night during Ramadan, as Friday is a holy day in Islam. In those months, Des underwent a journey of self-discovery. He gradually found himself no longer thinking of the locals as Muslims and him as a Christian, or even as a foreigner. In time, he concluded that he was just one person living among other people.

He was dazzled by how natural the villagers were and by the simplicity of the Islamic faith. He realised that he and those who lived in the *barrio* had so many similarities that the basis for dialogue and for understanding other faiths had always been there. He just hadn't known how to look for it before.

Learning a new language didn't come easily to him, so he learned Maranao slowly and steadfastly, eventually developing a proficiency in the language after about eight or nine months, which made him a novelty among local children who were not used to seeing white, Irish men who could speak their language.

There were those who believed Des wanted to convert to Islam, of course. When it was apparent that this was not happening, they thought he might try to convert them to Christianity. Some, having seen his respect for Islam, openly tried to talk him into becoming a Muslim, but none of these conversations distracted the priest from the true purpose of the exercise. Instead, he used these opportunities to explain how Christians could live in harmony with Muslims.

For many months there was no way of knowing whether his assimilation into Islamic life was a success or whether he was simply being tolerated as a curiosity. However, this lingering uncertainty disappeared when the local men started asking him about 'his brother' Lawan, specifically using the word *pagari*, which means brother or sister in the extended family. Des, who in the beginning did not realise the significance of the wording, would reply, 'Ah, he's fine.' But he soon saw he had forged a genuine friendship, akin to brotherhood, with Lawan and his family.

This bond was perhaps best demonstrated by his acceptance as a babysitter to Lawan's children. On occasion, when Lawan and his wife would travel to the city of Zamboanga to buy goods, they would leave Des in charge of the children, including their daughters. These acts, which showed how much they trusted Des, were not usual in their society.

The priest stayed with Lawan and his family for one year, after which time the house next door was offered for sale. Des interpreted this as a sign to stay in the *barrio* and continue his work, so he purchased the property. The acquisition also made practical sense, as more and more of his friends had begun visiting the *barrio*, but he didn't have a place for them to stay. Moving next door wouldn't break what he now considered to be a precious connection with Lawan and his family.

It was a small wooden house with two small rooms in poor condition. The roof of the toilet was almost completely gone, so users had to bring an umbrella inside when it rained.

One of the first people to visit him was a young student of Mindanao State University called Venus Guibone, who later became a Columban lay missionary. She went to the *barrio* as part of a team of three preparing to host a pre-confirmation seminar for grade six pupils (aged 11–12). They stayed in Des's house. Des gave his room to Basilio, the only male in the team, and he moved back in with Lawan.

Venus was struck by Des's simplicity, humility and great missionary spirit. He was an excellent host. He offered to draw water from the well, which she promptly declined as she was used to looking after herself. He looked after them extremely well – he personally put on their pillowcases and went on his bicycle to the market to get snacks for them, bringing back Maranao delicacies *dudol* and *tiateg* (types of rice cake), and bottles of Coke.

Although this was her first time meeting Des, she felt at home with him right away because of his gentle, no-frills, no-fuss approach to life. It was to be the beginning of a long working relationship. The visit deeply impacted Venus, who was only twenty-one years old at the time; she was inspired by his ability to live simply and in the midst of Muslims, yet remain committed to the Christians who lived in the area. It was her first time to witness this type of ministry, as she had grown up in a predominantly Christian environment.

Des remained in Bauyan for a few more months before an unexpected event forced his departure and return to Ireland: his mother, Alice, had died suddenly on 18 December 1981.

His legacy in the village lived on, however. The house he'd purchased was given to a Carmelite nun, Sister Rosa Fulleros, and later to an Irish Columban priest, Terry Twohig, who moved to the *barrio* and followed in Des's footsteps, living peacefully as Christians in a Muslim community.

CHAPTER 4

The best and most beautiful things in the world cannot be seen or
even touched – they must be felt with the heart.

Helen Keller

In 1980, another Irish Columban priest, Fr Michael 'Rufus'
Halley, joined the prelature of St Mary's in Marawi. Rufus had
already spent over ten years working in the Philippines. He and
Des had been friends since their student days in Dalgan Park
and, when the opportunity arose, they would meet at the central
house in Manila and catch up on each other's news.

Rufus's vocation to the poor made him stand out among his
peers. He always supported the underdog and felt great sympathy
for the island's Muslim population, whom he saw as a minority
in their own country. Whenever he and Des met, he asked about
the violence in Mindanao and was genuinely concerned by it.
The city of Marawi was in crisis, and he was drawn to it and to
the work of the prelature. He saw his place there, helping to heal
divisions between Muslims and Christians.

Rufus was different from most of the other Columbans.
He had grown up in a wealthy household in Co. Waterford
in Ireland and had enjoyed a privileged upbringing. He was
educated in Glenstal Abbey, a boarding school, and took part in
lots of sports, including horse-riding and rugby. He was never
comfortable with his family's wealth, however, and in 1962 he
entered the training college for the Missionary Society of St
Columban in Dalgan Park.

He stood out immediately as a sportsman. He could pick
up any bat, hurley stick or ball, and his friends in the seminary

knew he would beat them at every game. But these differences were only superficial. According to his friends, Rufus was not a studious student until he reached his final year, at which point he decided to apply himself to his academic work.

He entered the seminary in a year that the Catholic Church was going through an enormous upheaval, with the establishment of the Second Vatican Council in October 1962. Pope John XXIII convened bishops from all around the world to shape the Catholic Church for the modern age. Vatican II, as it became known, altered many areas of the church. Two of the biggest changes brought about by the council affected most Catholics. One was that Mass would from then on be celebrated in the local language of the country rather than Latin. A second was that the priest would now face the congregation during Mass.

Rufus's class questioned decisions and felt a loosening of the rules that had been part of seminary training since the first Vatican Council was established in 1869–70. The class was due to be ordained on 21 December 1968, but because they questioned everything and were considered rebellious by their superiors, the director told them in the summer of 1968 that they would not be ordained that year.[1] This clampdown caused great insecurity for the class, and it also caused tensions to rise among Columbans around the world. On returning after Christmas, however, the class was informed that it would be ordained on Easter Sunday, 6 April 1969.

In October 1969, Rufus travelled to the Philippines, along with classmates Peter O'Neill, Seán McDonagh, Donal Hogan and Shay Cullen. He was first assigned to Silang in Cavite, a parish south of Manila, the Philippine capital. He was to work alongside a number of older priests and Rufus was noticeably different from them. For one, he resisted any attempt to control his free spirit. He didn't allow people's opinions to change his behaviour. He socialised with the locals and enjoyed their company. He had a broad smile, a pale complexion and, in his younger days, bright ginger hair which had earned him the childhood nickname that lasted his whole life – Rufus.[2] The Filipinos were fascinated with his red hair and he instantly stood out everywhere he went.

From his first week of learning Tagalog (the language of Manila and parts of the northern Philippines), he spoke to everyone. He always laughed and joked, mixing as easily with older people as he did with children. He wasn't afraid of making mistakes, and many of his Irish friends envied his ease and lack of fear.

He remained in Silang for about four years, as it was common for the Columbans in those days to spend four years on each assignment. It was here, while working as a priest, that he mastered Tagalog. This was his first time living outside Ireland and also of seeing real poverty. He immersed himself in learning about the culture. He also started to develop an interest in Marxism as he spent time with people who believed it may be a route to a more just society.

He often spoke to his brother John about the Marxist liberation theology during those early years, but by the end of his first term he was less enamoured with it as he said they 'stopped caring to share [in] the full burden of poverty', with many of his Marxist friends eating out in fancy restaurants while talking about injustices in society.[3]

Rufus was assigned to Jala-Jala in 1975, a peninsula in Laguna Lake, located to the southeast of Manila. He demonstrated his commitment to the area's poor by living among them in the *barrio* rather than in the parish house. Rufus felt that the *convento*, the local term for the parish house, was too luxurious; although it was simple by Western standards, it was far more luxurious than the nipa and bamboo houses of the poor in the *barrios*. As far as he was concerned, he didn't want any barriers between himself and the poor.

This act, which he saw as liberating, was not meant as a slight to other Columbans, although many of his superiors felt he was upsetting the traditional hierarchy of the priests and their parishioners. No other Columban had done this, so some interpreted this decision as a comment on the lifestyle of other Columbans.

His commitment to the poor overshadowed his concern about the feelings of his fellow priests, however; his personal mission and dedication came before everything else. In time, his dedication to living among the poor often led him to sleep in shacks and huts. In Jala-Jala he quickly established a working style he would maintain all his life, which would further mark him apart from his fellow missionaries. Those who were close to him described him as a radical or maverick. His friends say they never met anyone more willing to expose himself to other people's problems, more reluctant to accept personal gratitude, or more disdainful of the excesses of wealth.

It would be impossible to understand Rufus without first understanding the influences that shaped his faith. His devil-may-care attitude to authority had its roots in the writings of Charles de Foucauld, a French priest who lived with the Tuareg nomads of the Saharan deserts of Algeria at the beginning of the twentieth century. De Foucauld was born in Strasbourg on 15 September 1858 and grew up in a wealthy family. When he was six years old, he and his sister, Marie, were orphaned and entrusted to the care of their grandfather, Colonel de Morlet. The significance of his parents' death manifested when de Foucauld reached his teenage years, as he became a difficult boy and lost his faith.

In 1876, he entered the Saint-Cyr Military Academy, from which he graduated as an army officer. Upon graduating, de Foucauld was sent to Algeria and Tunisia, which at the time were two French territories. In 1882, he left the military to explore Morocco. It was there, in the unlikeliest of places, that he rediscovered his faith.

De Foucauld was inspired by the religious dedication of Muslims he met while travelling. The encounters, which he later wrote about, made him question his own beliefs, or lack thereof.[4] He returned to Catholicism in October 1886, when he was twenty-eight years old. His faith strengthened and deepened until eventually, at the age of forty-three, he was ordained in Viviers in France.

He returned to the Sahara in Algeria, where he chose to live a solitary life. He travelled in southern Algeria and lived in Tamanrasset among the Tuareg, a nomadic race of Muslim pastoralists. Of the time he spent in their company, de Foucauld wrote that he had wanted to be among those who were 'the furthest removed, the most abandoned' from society.[5] The solitude and poverty of the Sahara in which the Tuareg eked out an existence appealed to de Foucauld. He shared their life and hardships, and suffered the elements with them. He studied the Berber-speaking nomads, compiling a written study of their language and cultural traditions, and a dictionary of their words and sayings. The monk adapted well to the conditions of the desert and had little difficulty relating to the world the Tuareg inhabited.

Despite dedicating his life to peace, de Foucauld was murdered by Bedouin gunmen on the evening of 1 December 1916 outside his compound at Tamanrasset. The killing occurred against a backdrop of anti-French sentiments that had grown in some North African countries.

Over fifty years later, in another remote part of the world, Rufus saw himself as someone who was following in de Foucauld's footsteps by choosing to live with the poor and alienated. He believed in de Foucauld's teachings and wanted to experience the uncertain future that the poor of Mindanao faced each day. He wanted to walk in their shoes, share their pain, experience their emotions and see life through their eyes, particularly through the eyes of the Muslim population.

When he first moved to the Philippines, he had decided to make a concerted effort not just to break down the barriers between the clergy and the parishioners, but to dismantle them so they could never be erected again. For a start, he asked not to be called 'Father'; instead he instructed his parishioners to call him 'Rufo', an abbreviation of his nickname. Furthermore, he tried not to pontificate or lecture from the altar. Some say he saw himself as an activist within the community. He helped local farmers to plant rice and he played basketball with local children. When he ate in the company of the poor, he followed local customs and used his hands instead of cutlery. He was also one of the first Columbans to go out and physically live in a *barrio*, doing any necessary travelling by motorcycle.

De Foucauld's influence on Rufus was clear, but his beliefs were as much rooted in politics as they were in the monk's writings. In 1972, a few years after his arrival and at a time when martial law was declared, Rufus met Louie Jalandoni, a revolutionary and former priest from Negros, who worked in solidarity with farmworkers and the poor to help them become free from abusive landowners and corrupt government officials in Negros. Rufus was working with a group of foreign missionaries who were studying the Philippine situation. They were discussing its history, along with the people's struggle for national and social liberation, when Jalandoni joined them one evening. During their discussions, Jalandoni explained how he had to go underground to avoid arrest by President Marcos's troops. At the end of the evening, Rufus took him aside and said, 'Louie, if you ever need a place to stay in, you will be welcome at my place. But not only you, others in your group who may need such a place, they too will be welcome.'[6]

A steady stream of political refugees who were on the wanted list of Marcos's dictatorship took sanctuary in Rufus's home after that night, and no matter how austere his surroundings were, he always made his guests feel immediately at home.

***

In the late 1970s, civil unrest was a feature of life in the Philippines. The MNLF started to break up as its founder, Nur Misuari, began to spend more and more of his time in Libya and Iran. At Mecca in 1977, Hashim Salamat was elected as the new chairperson of the MNLF. He accused Misuari of being secretive and authoritative and moving the MNLF away from Islamic ideals to be closer to communism. Misuari rejected the election and expelled Salamat from the organisation. Salamat then set up what was called the 'New MNLF Leadership'.[7] Salamat later renamed the organisation the Moro Islamic Liberation Front (MILF). He wanted the rebels to remain rooted in Islam and he also felt the name change emphasised his group's intention to disassociate itself from the MNLF.

Salamat saw the MILF as a religious movement, and cate-gorised the MNLF as a secular movement. He said, 'The two Fronts differ in ideology and objectives. The MILF strictly fol-lows the Islamic line and its objective of waging *jihad fi sabillah* (just fight for the sake of Allah) to make supreme the word of Allah and to establish an Islamic government.'[8] The MNLF was fighting for autonomy whereas the MILF wanted to establish an Islamic government and wage a war to achieve this objective. The armed forces of the MILF are known as the Bangsa Moro Islamic National Army (BINA) and the Bangsa Moro Islamic Armed Forces (BIAF).[9] Other people left the MNLF to set up a militant Muslim group called Mujahideen Commando Freedom Fighters, also known as Abu Sayyaf.[10]

It was against this background that the prelature of Marawi was trying to establish peaceful relations between Muslims and Christians at grass-roots level. Rufus was probably attracted to the work of Tudtud's prelature because it was similar to the work of de Foucauld in North Africa, particularly in how they both recommended immersion into another culture. Perhaps he saw the prelature's work in Marawi as something that combined both political and pastoral work. He began visiting the prelature and would occasionally say Mass at the chapel in Mindanao State University (MSU), which was run by the Columbans, who also looked after the pastoral and religious care of the Christian students there.

Education in Muslim-dominated areas had been lacking in the Philippines, so the MSU was established in 1961 to redress the balance. It was established as an educational institution where Muslims and Christians could study together. It represented the front line in the war against sectarianism, as it was predominantly a Muslim university attended by a handful of Christians, many of whom were attracted to the college because they were not required to pay tuition fees. It worked very well as an educational institution where members of both religions worked and studied side by side.

During the Mass at MSU, Rufus delivered the homily completely in Tagalog. He loved languages and communicating with people. His delivery was so strong he shocked some members of the congregation to the point that they stopped listening to what he was saying and started talking and whispering throughout the service, wondering about this white man who could speak their language so well.

Celia Eco was a member of the congregation during one of these homilies, and the sermon impacted her greatly. As she sat listening, she was deeply moved by the priest who seemed to be more Filipino than the Filipinos themselves. She turned to her friend Venus Guibone, who had previously spent a few days serving with Des in Bauyan.

'Who is this man? Where does he come from? Can you believe his Tagalog is so perfect?' she whispered.

'I don't know,' Venus replied. 'But he speaks Tagalog almost better than I do.'

There is no doubt that Rufus took pleasure in speaking the language so well. In fact, his friends said he would perform facial gymnastics in order to pronounce words correctly. He would sometimes preach in a mixture of Tagalog and English with such mastery that some students would remark aloud, 'My God, I've never heard of that term before.'

In 1980, Rufus left Jala-Jala and moved officially to the prelature of Marawi, where he was made assistant chaplain at MSU, assisting fellow Irish Columban and classmate Fr Seán McDonagh in his ministerial duties.

In the beginning, Rufus was a reluctant chaplain to the students. He wasn't an academic and didn't feel comfortable in a university, preferring practical work to theoretical studies. This, of course, immediately made the students warm to him and he was readily accepted by them. He was introduced to Venus and Celia, and they struck up an instant rapport. Celia was working in the university's chemistry laboratory and was actively involved in the chaplaincy, where she worked with Venus. One day Venus approached Rufus after Mass and addressed him as 'Padre'.

'Please, call me Popong! That's my Filipino name,' Rufus said. 'Bishop Tudtud gave it to me and all my friends call me by it.'[11]

Soon after that, Rufus started organising soccer tournaments in the university, and he became popular with the male students, regardless of their religion, because of this. He blended in with the students, using his easy manner and charm to build bridges between the communities and, in time, he came to understand why he had been sent to the university.

**

On 17 January 1981, President Marcos ended martial law. Given that the 1973 constitution enacted by Marcos had removed the limitations of the presidential term, Marcos was then able to run in his third presidential election. It was held in June 1981 and, as there were no strong candidates to oppose him, he was re-elected.

Two years later, one of Marcos's challengers, Senator Benigno Aquino, whom he had exiled from the country in 1980, decided to return to the Philippines. Aquino was assassinated when he landed at Manila International Airport on 21 August 1983. Marcos's government was blamed for the assassination and the incident was to have disastrous and far-reaching effects on the Philippines' international image. Tourism levels plunged dramatically, damaging an economy that was already weak. The country's foreign debt had reached such heights that a substantial portion of its annual income was needed just to repay the interest on these loans. It was believed that Marcos had been more interested in lining his own pockets than rebuilding a nation. Under his reign, the country's debt rose from $8.2 billion in 1977 to $24.4 billion in 1982.[12]

The Columbans could do nothing but watch alongside the Filipino people, who continued to suffer under a corrupt regime.

During this tumultuous period, Rufus was working as a shop assistant in a Muslim grocery store in Marawi. This was a huge step in helping build relationships between him and local Muslims, as the shop owner trusted him to handle the cash and look after the store. It also helped him learn Maranao. He wanted to get involved with local people as an equal and be able to converse with them about the matters of the day. Although it wasn't intentional, once again Rufus succeeded in unsettling those around him. Many of his colleagues, including some Muslim leaders, felt it was beneath a priest to be seen working in a grocery store. But Rufus was undeterred and continued to work there, building relationships and friendships that would last his whole lifetime.

The friendships he formed with Celia and Venus during his time in MSU also lasted his lifetime. One of the qualities that attracted Venus to him was that he was never afraid of being emotionally intimate with people. Rufus wasn't afraid to be close to anyone, even though he was a priest.

One day Venus visited him on her way to see a friend in Marawi city. She called into his house, the parish rectory, unsure if he was home. When she arrived she met the cook, who asked her to carry lunch in to him as he was bedridden with a knee injury. He was lying in bed with a bandage and cast around his left leg, and although he was delighted and surprised to see Venus, she noticed he looked weak and down.

'Venus, I'm so happy you called by! Are you going to stay the night or are you just passing through?'

'I can stay. I also want to visit some other friends and the Sisters here. Can we talk later, maybe before supper?'

'Absolutely!'

'What happened to your knee?'

'Ah, I don't know. It seems to be some kind of TB in my

knee. It needs surgery – they think it could be related to some past injury from playing soccer. It's very painful, though, and makes it hard to sleep.'

Later that evening, Venus and Rufus discussed a student from the university who was going through a hard time. He told Venus that the student was in her third year of college and had become pregnant. She had approached Rufus looking for support and advice. She was the eldest child in a poor family; her parents were very strict and wanted her to have a better life by receiving a good education. Rufus found out the man she was involved with was married and posted in Marawi with the military.

Rufus counselled the distraught girl to share her situation with a peer she could trust, as he knew he wouldn't be able to journey with her the way a woman would. Rufus asked Venus if she would be her female confidante. He arranged for the girls to meet at the Catholic chapel, where Venus pledged confidentiality and moral support. Later the student agreed to bring two other friends into her small circle of support.

They managed to keep her pregnancy a secret until the semester was over. Rufus would meet with them occasionally and remind them of the sacredness of trust and confidence. Venus felt it was as if she suddenly grew up overnight. Rufus's capacity to trust the girls and to take them seriously helped them deal with the new experience in a positive way. At the end of the semester, Rufus found shelter for the pregnant girl in a nun's place where her friends could visit.

The four girls graduated in the same year. Venus stayed in Marawi to teach in the university, while the two friends and confidantes returned to their villages. The girl had her baby, and Rufus continued to support her financially after she gave birth. She nominated Venus, Rufus and the other friends as godparents to the baby and Rufus supported her as she prepared to reunite with her family and present the baby to them. Venus experienced Rufus's compassion, alongside his deep sense of justice, during this period. She saw how his heart was filled with love and joy, and she felt blessed to be his friend.

Celia and Rufus's friendship was also deepening. They were both strongly drawn to the spirit of God, and often discussed how to keep the Mass more alive, which was something that concerned Rufus greatly. One day, they met up to talk about how to dramatise the gospel, when, out of the blue, Rufus asked her if she had ever thought about becoming a nun.

Celia laughed and said, 'I thought we were here to discuss the gospel?'

'We are, Cel, but seriously ... have you ever considered that you may have another calling, other than being a lay person?'

'Yes, Popong. I've often thought about it, and in fact I have written to three religious orders that don't use veils. You know I couldn't stand to wear a veil ... but I wasn't happy with their replies.'

'Well, I can recommend one more to you,' he said.

He went on to tell her about the Little Sisters of Jesus, a religious order that follows the teachings and spirituality of Charles de Foucauld. At that time, he was reading a book about the Little Sisters. 'Write to them!' he urged her.

Celia liked to make up her own mind, so she refused to write to them simply because Rufus had suggested it. Each time they met, however, Rufus would greet her with, 'Well, did you write yet?'

She eventually gave in and sent a letter, and he was very happy and excited when she subsequently started corresponding in earnest with the order. Celia decided to investigate the path of becoming a nun further, so she spent an observation period of around a year with the Little Sisters of Jesus. She stayed away from Rufus during this time because he was so impressed with them that she didn't want him to influence her final decision.

The next time they saw each other, Celia confessed she was still undecided. She was completely taken aback when Rufus advised her to go on a retreat to contemplate her direction. She had been so sure he was going to direct her towards joining the Little Sisters that she didn't quite know how to react, but she followed his advice and went on a retreat. To her surprise, she discovered it was just what she needed. She realised she was drawn to the Little Sisters and joined them in 1982.

At the same time, as part of his immersion process, Rufus moved to a small *barrio* near Karomatan to develop his Maranao and then, a year later, he went to Louvain-la-Neuve in Belgium to study Islam with the Jesuits.

CHAPTER 5

I destroy my enemies when I make them my friends.

Abraham Lincoln

In 1983, Bishop Tudtud asked Fr Des to move to Marawi city. The city's population was approximately ninety-eight per cent Muslim and there was a lot of tension between the army (which was regarded as Christian) and the Muslims. Officially called the Islamic City of Marawi, the city was built on the shores of Lake Lanao, the second largest and deepest lake in the Philippines. The people of Marawi are known as Maranaos, 'the people of the lake', and the city landscape and its inhabitants were quite different from the cities Des had lived in before. The Maranao women wore malongs, traditional Maranao Muslim attire which is similar to a sarong, and the predominant sound was of people speaking in Maranao, while the daily calls to prayer from sixty-five mosques echoed throughout the city.

Des moved into Tudtud's house, which sat on top of the hill in Marawi. The house was a converted school building and it was common to see lizards running along the walls. Tudtud was an inspiring person and helped to keep Des and his colleagues upbeat during difficult times. The more violence that occurred, however, the more difficult it became to remain upbeat. There were daily shootings. Des often found that they would be making progress and beginning to rebuild relationships, when somebody would be killed and they would almost have to start the whole process all over again.

He got straight to work, immersing himself in the Muslim community, spending a lot of time visiting the various groups in the prelature. It was a very different situation to the *barrio* of Bauyan, which had been rural, relaxed and peaceful.

The Carmelite Sisters also joined the prelature in 1983 and opened a monastery to enrich the contemplative aspect of the mission. Des welcomed their arrival and found them to be a great support, as one of their specific purposes was to pray for the unity of Muslims and Christians and for good relations between the two communities.

He settled into a rhythm and was beginning to enjoy his mission. About a year later, while he was visiting a colleague in Karomatan, he was introduced to the local sultan, Maguid Maruhom, whose brother, Abdul Ceher, had lived next door to Des when he lived in Bauyan. Abdul told his brother about Des, who was known as a good man among the Muslims in the *barrio*. They were friends and Des had often lent Abdul his motorbike.

When Maguid heard about Des, he was immediately intrigued. As far as he was aware, it was the first time an Irish priest had lived with a Muslim family in Mindanao, and Maguid couldn't understand why a priest would choose to live with a sultan in a Muslim-dominated area. He wanted to know more.

Maguid had received good feedback from other tribes about Des, particularly from the Tabligh religious fraternity, one of the many different Islamic groups on the island of Mindanao.[1] Maguid tried to discover the reasons behind his stay. He asked one of the Carmelite Missionary Sisters, Sister Rosa, who told him that Des wanted to immerse himself in the Muslim culture to gain an understanding of it, to learn the local dialect and to learn about the Muslim community. When Maguid eventually met Des, he asked him about his views on Muslim–Christian relations and about his vision of peace, justice and community.

As they got to know each other better, Maguid questioned the wisdom of Des staying in a Muslim community. But Des told him about the vision of the church, and explained its new thinking. Maguid believed Des was sincere – though he wasn't convinced it was worthwhile for Des to take the risk and expose himself to danger just to learn about the culture and language. After all, Marawi was notorious among the Muslim community for being a dangerous place. Maguid advised Des to abandon his way of thinking.

Despite warnings of this kind, Des continued to work hard in dialogue. He got involved in the Dansalan Research Center in Marawi, which ran an education programme for Christians about Muslims and Islam. The research centre often hosted seminars, and Des was very active in this programme. He worked with Islamic religious leaders and forged long-lasting friendships. One person who became a particularly close friend was Professor Moctar Matuan; both men gave seminars on Muslim Filipino culture and customs, and often spoke during the summer programmes, which were designed for professional church workers preparing for ministries in countries where Islam was dominant.

Although the theory behind the prelature was well conceived, Des found himself struggling with deep-rooted prejudice daily. Many of the Christians in his community had family members who had died in the ongoing sectarian violence; in some areas where the fighting was continuous, people were killed every week. In the immediate aftermath of such violence, Des knew to withdraw the offer of talks. He couldn't say, 'Let's go into dialogue.' People needed time to heal the wounds and to work through their own hatred. Des was experienced enough to give people that space and time, and then he would gently approach the topic of dialogue and reconciliation.

***

Bishop Tudtud was Des's touchstone during this period and a guiding light when difficult situations arose, until a terrible tragedy occurred on 27 June 1987. Tudtud was flying from Manila to Baguio city, around 250 kilometres north of Manila, when the plane he was travelling on crashed into Mount Ugo in Benguet. All fifty people on board were killed.

Tudtud's death was a huge loss to the people of the prelature, which now felt leaderless. Through his grief, Des continued his work in dialogue with the Muslim community as best he could, trying to keep things going on a day-to-day basis. Archbishop Fernando Capalla was appointed the temporary apostolic administrator while the church looked for a replacement for Tudtud.

Helping the Christians to overcome their own prejudice and fear was part of Des's mission, and it was something he persevered with through the turmoil after Tudtud's death. Soon, however, he unexpectedly found himself having to deal with his own fear. He was visiting a Christian woman in her hair salon in the city, which was located on a busy main street. They sat near the window, out of which he occasionally looked during the conversation. He didn't notice anything amiss with the hectic cityscape as they spoke.

Once finished with the visit, he said goodbye to his parishioner and promised to call again. Returning to his car he noticed the windows were open but thought nothing of it. As he sat into the front seat, a man came around from behind the car and put a gun to his head. Des thought they wanted the keys of the car and feared that they would shoot him and then throw him out of the car before making their getaway. It was only when another fellow jumped into the passenger seat beside him, and a third appeared from behind with a gun, that Des realised this was more than an opportunistic car-jacking.

'Don't shoot! Don't shoot me!' he implored his would-be kidnappers, raising his hands in the air.

The woman he had been talking to came out of her salon and saw what was happening. She started screaming hysterically and her screams attracted a crowd. People began to gather around. It was the middle of the day and there were quite a few people on the street. The attackers panicked and decided to withdraw. They ran away from the car, and Des, seeing his opportunity, took off like a flash in the other direction. He drove straight back to his house. He was overcome by fear and was angry with the men for instilling this panic in him, but he was also angry at his own weakness in being afraid.

After the attack, it took Des some time to work through his apprehension, but he knew he couldn't stay in Marawi if he was living in constant fear. He felt so powerless living as part of a minority, and his sense of vulnerability was heightened for a long time. During this period he drew on what he had learned from Bishop Tudtud.

Through contemplation he realised that this was also part of the dialogue and part of the vision Tudtud had brought to the region. It's only when you live in vulnerability that you start to trust others. Trust is not generated from a position of power. When someone is in a position of weakness and needs others, dialogue is always much more possible. With this in mind, he began to feel more relaxed about moving around again. Eventually, he was able to put the incident behind him completely.

CHAPTER 6

The conflict in Mindanao is not a 'Muslim Problem'.
It is a Philippine Problem.

Bishop Bienvenido Tudtud

In 1987 Rufus returned to a Philippines that was facing political unrest and a general election. He was assigned to Balabagan, where he joined Fr Kevin McHugh, a priest from Ireland who had been working in the parish since 1983. While Rufus had been attracted to the prelature for the Muslim apostolate, Kevin was there principally to serve the Christian community. Kevin was inspired to volunteer to work with Christians who lived within the wider Muslim community after he read a book by Steve Clarke called *Building Christian Communities*. In 1977, he went to Malabang for what he thought would be only two weeks but found himself still in the area in Balabagan ten years later. Kevin found Rufus easy to live with, and they were relaxed companions.

Both men kept in touch with other Columbans, and news of Des's attempted kidnapping spread fast among them. The priests were advised to take care while travelling around. In November 1987, Rufus addressed these concerns in a letter to Celia:

> I'm back in Balabagan for the past 5 weeks. So near yet so far. We had a Columban meeting in Cagayan [de Oro] the past few days, and a prelature retreat this coming week in Bethania so I have stayed this weekend here in Cagayan.
>
> I went to Marawi on Friday to see the Carmelites and

all the team including Lady Di [Sr Dylene]. They are all in great form T.G. [thank God] in spite of the uncertain situation.

You know that Des was almost kidnapped two weeks ago. He is naturally a bit anxious, so you might remember him/us all (I know you do). This fear I certainly know at times and it's not so pleasant. The whole situation and our somewhat helplessness just emphasizes the point of letting go completely and letting Him take over.[1]

Rufus went on to speak about becoming self-aware, and his journey towards knowing himself better:

I'm learning more and more about myself all the time and it's just so fuelling. The truth, as somebody so rightly said, will make you free, but it will first make you miserable. Life for me now is much more than a pilgrimage – it is really an odyssey. With a pilgrimage you must come aware of the facts beforehand, such as where you are going and more or less how and when you are going to get there. Whereas with an odyssey, there is joy, anticipation and awareness in this going, but where it is going to lead or when we will arrive or what will happen only Himself knows.

This past six/seven weeks Balabagan is pretty peaceful T.G. and long may it continue old friend. I am going to try [to] find a small part-time job in a store when I go back (a bit like in Marawi with Acud). I hope I can get one so please say a special speed delivery to Himself. It would be great for the Maranao and dialogue through immersion.

The letter from Rufus reflects the deep friendship he had developed with Celia over the years. In fact, they were so close to each other that she had been reprimanded by the Little Sisters over her friendship with him when she first joined the order.

Celia noticed their relationship had been slowly evolving into a deeper friendship. She knew Rufus was struggling with himself, and she believed he continued to struggle, as his role as a priest was clashing with his personal and human side. She was also struggling in her role as a sister, so it was something she understood well. He told her he had to be a unique kind of priest, different from the others; he would be a liberated priest who broke the rules. He explained to her that it was okay to feel human, with all the challenges that brought.

When they met for the first time after he returned from his travels in Europe, Celia was so excited to see him that she was worried she wouldn't be able to stop herself from hugging him. She secretly prayed she would be alone when she saw him again for the first time. To her delight, her prayers were answered, and there was nobody else in the house when he arrived. He enveloped her in a bear hug, beaming with joy at seeing his old friend.

Soon, they became freer in showing affection to each other. Sometimes it was by hugging; other times, when he felt weighed down by something, he would ask her to hold his hand. As well as writing regularly, he would call her occasionally, particularly if he wanted to share some recent experience, usually of a spiritual nature. He always ended his call with 'Can I give you a hug over the phone, Celia?' and he would make a sound like he was hugging her. After the first time he 'hugged' her on the phone, Celia wrote to him:

> Popong, you know I really could not give you a hug over the phone because it was a bit strange but what I really wanted to do was to hold your hand and to touch your face.[2]

But when she saw him next, Celia found herself overcome with embarrassment and didn't raise the issue of hugging him. That night she travelled with him in a jeepney (a popular means of public transport) to the bus, and she noticed that even though there were other passengers with them, he wasn't self-conscious at all and talked about himself and about his fears. He didn't care that other people could hear. She loved this about him and wished she could learn to be just as free. As he got onto the bus for Balabagan, he gave her another hug that kept her warm long after he had left.

Celia knew Rufus was afraid and this made her fear for him, particularly since Des's attempted kidnapping. In the early years when he first arrived in Marawi, he developed a bad case of diarrhoea. The doctor told him he had an infection, but when he met Celia he told her that was not really the problem. The problem was that he was very, very afraid. The constant threat of kidnapping troubled him, but Celia learned later that despite this fear, he would go to places against advice, walking through dangerous parts of Marawi to visit Muslim families. She knew he wouldn't change his habits, despite these warnings. That night, as his bus departed, she said a quick prayer that he would arrive safely.

***

Back in Balabagan, Kevin observed Rufus's absolute dedication to a life of prayer. Kevin knew that many of his fellow priests went through periods when their dedication to prayer was stronger than others, but for Rufus it was a way of life. Kevin would hear the creaking of the stairs every morning at 5 a.m. as Rufus went to the chapel and spent an hour in silent prayer with the Lord. Kevin often joined him for evening prayer.

They built a small adoration chapel in Balabagan, and Rufus

insisted on keeping it absolutely simple. He wanted a very basic tabernacle at eye level, without any flowers or candles. He believed in simplicity because it brought out the essence of prayer.

A few months after Rufus moved to Balabagan, Peter O'Neill, who had become the district superior of Mindanao, decided to visit him. Some of the roads around Balabagan were only reachable by boat; it was a very remote, small village so it was a long trip, involving travelling by bus and boat. Peter thought Rufus would be excited to see him and they'd spend the day swimming, but after lunch Rufus said, 'I'm off to work.'

Peter was amazed that Rufus would leave him while he was visiting, but he soon realised that not much got in the way of Rufus's work, whether it was visiting parishioners or working in the local school. Kevin noticed Peter's disappointment, so the two of them played hurling for the rest of the afternoon on the beach. Except for the sunshine and the intense heat, for those brief few hours Peter felt he could almost be back in Ireland.

On other occasions Kevin and Rufus would go out to the Lorenzo plantation, which was named after a prominent landowner family who were politically active. The Lorenzos were very good to the Columbans and, in the early years, often invited the priests for a meal and a movie. They had an airstrip and a place where people could swim. Kevin and Rufus would go out occasionally and play hurling. Rufus was a fantastic athlete and was deadly accurate at hurling. He had been a goalkeeper for the team in Dalgan Park.

They were glorious days for both men. They would play and swim during the day, and spend the evening watching the sun set, looking over the water to the Baganian peninsula as the sun became red and then orange as it lowered in the sky. The glow after the sunset brought out the clouds in relief and at times they felt it was like heaven on earth.

'Here we are. Two free people, enjoying nature's bounty,' Rufus commented to Kevin. These evenings gave Rufus more happiness than anything else.

On one occasion, Rufus and Kevin were both on a plane to Cotabato city when they saw that the Rio Grande river had turned very brown as a result of deforestation. This infuriated Rufus. The rains had brought down the top soil from the hills and deposited it at the mouth of the river at Cotabato.

When they returned to Balabagan, Rufus immediately wrote four letters to prominent loggers. He prepared the letters well and was respectful throughout. Despite this, he managed to incur the wrath of one of them. He and his brother resented that Rufus had attempted to interfere with the logging business. Rufus heard that they were upset, but it didn't stop him from further action.

He next wrote to a landowner and political leader near Marawi. As well as writing letters, Rufus planted trees in the hills to counteract the wanton destruction of the forest. He always took action when he saw there was a problem and never held back when he felt it was his duty to act.

***

The Columbans continued to send young missionaries to the Philippines and, in August 1990, Fr Paul Glynn and Fr Brendan Kelly arrived at the Columban headquarters in Singalong Street in Manila. It was dark outside and pouring rain. They had been assigned to the Manila area, where they would remain for two years. When they arrived they didn't know anybody, or much about the Philippines in general.

As they walked into the dark, grey building, they whispered to each other about how depressing it looked. The secretary met them at the door and they introduced themselves. They were feeling disorientated and homesick, when Rufus just happened to come down the stairs. He greeted them with a big smile and a welcome.

'Hello, lads. You're very welcome. Great to see new people coming into this country!'

He brought them upstairs and gave them a cup of tea, all the while making them feel very comfortable with small talk and asking them news of home. He showed them how to use the air-conditioning system, as they'd never seen one before, and he was full of energy and excitement.

Brendan turned to Paul and said, 'If even half the Columbans are as nice as him, we'll be doing well in this country.'

Rufus told them he had managed to evade taking on the responsibilities of running the school and parish in Balabagan and had just finished living with a Muslim family there. They had a fruit and vegetable shop and he had lived and worked with them, immersing himself completely in their world. He also revealed, to their disappointment, that he was on his way to England, where he would spend the next few years helping out in a parish there, living in complete contrast to the world he was leaving.

CHAPTER 7

*Faith is taking the first step even when you
don't see the whole staircase.*

Martin Luther King Jr

Des remained in Marawi until the middle of 1988 when he was
elected to go to the Columban General Assembly in Pusan,
Korea. The general assembly is held every six years, usually in
a country where the Columbans are working. It deliberates on
Columban affairs, reviews the missions and evaluates various
commitments of the society, as well as making plans for the
coming years.

While in Korea, Des was elected to the central administration
of the Columbans, which was based in Ireland. Known within the
Columbans as the General Council, the administration consisted
of a superior general and four other Columban priests elected to
a six-year term to administer the Columban organisation around
the world. Des was delighted to have the opportunity to spend
some time in his homeland, and in November 1988 he moved
back to Ireland.

He adjusted well to working in the General Council. He had
been out of the country for twenty years and returning to Ireland
gave him a long-overdue opportunity to catch up with his family.
He was around for Christmases, family weddings and baptisms,
and it felt good to be part of these normal family occasions.

This normalcy did not last, however. Although he expected
to be based in Ireland until 1994, he was unexpectedly called
into the Papal Nuncio's office on the Navan Road in Dublin in
June 1991. He presumed the meeting had something to do with

the General Council, but when he arrived, the Papal Nuncio, Archbishop Emanuele Gerada, handed him a letter, which said the Holy Father, Pope John Paul II, had appointed him as apostolic administrator of Marawi.

This news was a complete shock and Des didn't quite know how he felt about it other than that he wasn't completely happy with the appointment. He was quite settled in Ireland and had been content to stay on for another few years. Des was also apprehensive about going back to Marawi, particularly in a leadership role. He knew he had strong leadership qualities but was worried he mightn't inspire people in the same way Bishop Tudtud had managed. Tudtud had been a very charismatic man, and he'd understood and connected with the local people in ways a foreigner couldn't. Des believed that appointing an outsider to the role of apostolic administrator was taking a backward step. He also felt he would find it difficult to keep Tudtud's vision alive. On top of that, on a personal level, he had difficulty adjusting to the thoughts of going back to live in Marawi and to placing himself, once again, in a position of vulnerability.

He took time to reflect on and pray about this new assignment. In the end he came to the decision that he should undertake the appointment with dedication and strength. Therefore, in October 1991, he pushed aside any remaining reservations and moved back to Marawi.

When he arrived in the city, he moved back into the house he had once shared with Bishop Tudtud. Many of the personnel were the same as when he had left. A lay missionary called Lydia Macas from Baloi in Lanao del Norte still lived in the bishop's house and looked after many aspects of promoting the work of the prelature. She was a versatile person who had multiple roles in the parish: coordinator of the catechists, parish worker, seminar facilitator, a member of the editorial staff of *Tindog* (the newsletter of the prelature, which Tudtud had started), and an anchor woman of the prelature's mini radio station, which Tudtud had also started. She was an important part of the team.

Venus Guibone was good friends with Lydia, as they both worked on *Tindog* (which means 'stand up') while she was in her final year in Mindanao State University. Lydia was a good communicator and a natural journalist, and often went with Venus to interview Maranaos at different times.

Civil unrest in Marawi was gradually increasing again, making life more difficult for Christians. Des found that counselling his parishioners and colleagues was a growing part of his new job, as they all sought to make it through the turbulent times.

He often visited the Carmelite Sisters to pray and to talk to them about the problems the parishioners were facing. The sisters lived only about two kilometres from his house, with the last 300 metres to their house accessible via an overgrown path. The house wasn't serviced by public transport, so if the sisters had a visitor, they would often go to the priests' house to get a lift.

Soon after Des returned, an American Trappist priest came to visit and Des brought him up to the nuns early in the morning. Later that afternoon, he collected the Trappist and two of the sisters to bring them into the city. Des was driving a jeepney, with the Trappist sitting next to him. The two nuns were sitting in the rear and, as they were driving down a secluded part of the road, two men wearing balaclavas jumped out of the bushes, carrying Armalite guns.

The bandits must have misjudged the speed the jeepney was travelling at, as by the time they jumped out from the undergrowth, the jeepney was already upon them. They shouted, 'Stop, stop!' at Des, but, feeling an overwhelming adrenaline rush, he accelerated instead of stopping. The armed men fired two shots directly at the vehicle and continued firing warning shots as it passed them, but Des still didn't stop. He kept his foot hard on the accelerator and drove as fast as possible until he got out of their range.

Once they got around the bend, about fifty metres down the road, Des allowed himself to breathe. His reaction had been completely spontaneous, and he realised afterwards that it might have been the most stupid thing he could have done, as they could have all been murdered. Thankfully, it turned out for the best. He notified the police immediately after the incident, but though they searched the area, the bandits were long gone.

Des eventually took the sisters home later that day. The Carmelite nuns were no strangers to terror; a number of years earlier some of the nuns had been kidnapped and held for ransom. It was the Catholic Church's policy to not pay ransom to kidnappers. It believed there would be no end to the kidnappings if it did. Victims usually didn't know what had happened to secure their release, but the suspicion among the religious orders was that the government or the local politicians paid the ransom as a publicity stunt because they wanted their photographs taken with the people who were kidnapped.

This was Des's second major encounter with an attempted abduction. It would not be his last.

***

Part of the reason for the violence in Mindanao was because corruption was rife in the political system. Elections, for example, had a long history of being violent in Mindanao. On 11 May 1992, Motalib Dimaporo, the incumbent mayor of Karomatan, was re-elected during a general election by a vast majority amid claims of cheating. He won through the use of threats and intimidation and by buying votes. Hadji Tumalding Calib, the opposing candidate, was subsequently shot dead. Many allege that he was killed by the Dimaporo clan so he would not be a threat to their power.

Traditionally, the violence didn't take place between Muslims and Christians during political campaigns; it was between different political groupings of Muslims. However, by the early 1990s, shrewd politicians were taking advantage of the increasing animosity between Muslims and Christians. During the 1992 campaign, about fifteen Christians were killed in Marawi, and an entire Maranao family was massacred in Palao, Iligan city. It was widely accepted that people on both sides were killed for political gain, however, rather than for their religious differences. But these deaths succeeded in what the masterminds behind them had set out to do: that is, to exacerbate the mistrust between Christians and Muslims.

Des watched on in horror as a whole series of retaliatory murders and attacks signalled the beginning of an uncontrolled spiral of violence. Along with Bishop Fernando Capalla of Iligan, Bishop Ledesma of Cagayan de Oro and colleagues in the prelature, Des began to call meetings with local religious leaders, the army and representatives of various Muslim groups to try to stem this violence.

Bishop Capalla, Des and some Maranao friends also went to Sultan Moctar Matuan's office in the Dansalan Research Center and asked him to call a meeting between representatives from the two communities.

'The situation is getting out of control, Moctar. What are we going to do?' Des asked.

'It's an urgent situation. We need to include as many people from the community as we can. I will send out a letter inviting people to meet. I can't promise they will respond, though,' Moctar replied.

In truth, Moctar didn't think many people would react to his call, so he was more than surprised when seventy people turned up at the first meeting. Clearly, for these people, the situation had reached a point of desperation; both Muslims and Christians felt forced to do something, to come together to find a solution because working separately was not having any effect. Des believed it was at this point that the dialogue really started to become meaningful for everyone; when they realised that neither group alone could bring about peace.

The dialogue that followed in a series of meetings was the beginning of a frank discussion and exchange of ideas between the Muslim and Christian communities. Both sides knew the violence and murders that were occurring were detrimental to all of them. The participants felt it was essential that they show leadership in their respective communities. These people from different backgrounds and religions all had one thing in common: they wanted the violence and the killings to stop.

Des believed it was at the time of greatest human vulnerability, when the people truly started relying on God rather than their own resources, that positive things started to happen.

Their efforts at keeping peace were tested in October 1992 when Sultan Naga Dimaporo was shot dead at the gate of the national mosque in Manila, the Golden Mosque. The Dimaporos immediately blamed the Iranuns (a Moro ethnic group) for the assassination, claiming it was a reprisal for Hadji Tumalding Calib's murder. The Maranaos tend to take revenge by killing the relatives of anyone they suspect of being involved in an attack, including up to fourth cousins – therefore many Iranuns began to flee their homeland forever, for fear of reprisals. Their homes and farms were quickly taken over by the Dimaporos, and the municipality of Karomatan was re-named Sultan Naga Dimaporo in honour of the late mayor. Des's friend, Maguid

Maruhom, was Calib's cousin and also an Iranun, so he, too, had to leave his home.

Part of the responsibility of those attending the meetings at this delicate time was to try to resolve any disputes among Muslims. When Maguid went into hiding, he tried to ask Governor Mahid Mutilan, the president of the Ulama League of the Philippines, to intervene in this row. Mutilan was also an aleem, or Islamic scholar, having graduated in theology from the Al-Azhar University in Cairo. He had spent eleven years as a missionary in Japan before returning to Lanao del Sur. Maguid had great admiration for him as he was the first ulama ever elected to a government position when he became the mayor of Marawi in 1988.

Maguid rang Mutilan several times but only managed to get through to the security guard. He wasn't willing to discuss his private business with him, so he rang the conference hall where a meeting was taking place and got through to the secretary.

'Can I speak to Governor Mutilan, please?'

'He's not available at the moment, but you can leave a message if you want,' she replied.

'No, I don't want to leave a message. I've already left several messages for him.'

Maguid found it difficult to contain his annoyance. He was aware that Des was also attending the meeting in the conference hall, and so he said, 'Let me speak to Father Des.'

When Des came to the phone, Maguid told him that he wanted to talk to Mutilan, but was having difficulty getting in touch with him.

'Well Maguid, why don't you meet me tomorrow?' Des offered. 'I could meet you at the *convento* of the cathedral. Can you be there at 12 p.m.? I have an hour free.'

'Yes, Father Des. Thank you. I can meet you tomorrow.'

'Great, I'm looking forward to seeing you,' Des said, before hanging up.

On his way to meet Des the next day, Maguid bought some dried squid to show his appreciation for Des's efforts, as he knew the Irishman had a penchant for fish. At the meeting, Des got straight to the point, asking why Maguid wanted to see Mutilan. He replied that he wanted his help.

'If you can trust me, can I not do something to help? Maybe I can talk to the Dimaporos or Mutilan himself?' Des suggested, in his typically quiet manner.

'You don't know our culture and we cannot do that. If you attempt that you might fail, or get in trouble, and I don't want that.'

'Think it over,' Des said. 'Don't answer now, and if you change your mind ring me.'

Maguid could not understand why Des wanted to get involved and help solve the problem. This was a *rido*, which is like a vendetta or retaliation; it means an eye for an eye, and can go on for generations. Christians should stay out of *ridos*, Maguid thought, as they were a part of the Maranao culture.

But Des seemed insistent in wanting to help.

Maguid frowned. 'It is rather odd for you to come in and help resolve the problem with the Dimaporos. It would be very difficult for you. I think the Dimaporos would need lots of blood money.'

'But what will you do, Maguid, if you don't resolve the problem with the Dimaporos? If you want to put the problem to the back of your mind, then you have no choice. Your religion teaches you to forgive. Maybe you should remember this. Unless you forgive, you cannot put this problem behind you.'

Maguid listened to this priest, his sincerity clear in his voice and expression. Leaning forward, he told Des he sometimes found it hard to talk with ulama, as they weren't always sincere. He said he heard one local ulama being asked by his people why he was talking with the Christian bishops at these meetings and the ulama replied, 'I'm a politician. You cannot blame me for this.'

When Maguid had heard this, he'd decided they weren't sincere in their approach to these cross-community meetings, so he felt there was no point in them. He also complained to Des about what was being ignored at these meetings. 'The dialogue is not addressing issues at grass-roots level; things like solving family disputes and tribal disputes. The forum gives the wrong impression and a promise for peace; that there is a unity between Muslims and Christians,' Maguid said. 'But some imams and ulama are fundamentalists, and they believe conflict is rooted in religion, in faith. As a result, the grass-roots level issues, like poverty, aren't being addressed at the meetings.'

'You're right,' Des said.

Maguid had something close to an epiphany in that moment. 'I will go to the grass-roots level myself and bring people together to make them understand each other.'

'Good!' Des simply replied. 'Do it.'[1]

Maguid was aware that he was full of anger, fear, frustration and pride in that moment, and it certainly wasn't easy for him to accept that he had to forgive the people he had fought with. There was a long history of violence and conflict between the families, and he had lost family members to the *rido*.

Furthermore, Maguid couldn't understand why the ulama had shown no interest in his problems, yet a Catholic priest was so concerned about him and his predicament. The priest was even encouraging him to act, and do what he felt the others were not doing.

Still fearful for his life because of the *rido*, Maguid moved to a poor community in Tukuran in west Mindanao. Some guests came to visit him in 1993. One of the girls was working with missionaries and she gave him a blank envelope. She said it had been sent by a white priest who knew Maguid, but she couldn't say what his name was. When Maguid opened the envelope it contained money and he knew that Des was looking out for him.

Maguid then moved to Manila for five or six months, where he lived with the Carmelite Sisters. He had to be so secretive about his movements that not even his wife knew where he was staying. He tried to blend in and pretend he wasn't a Muslim, so he learned how to lead the rosary and pray with the Catholics.

***

What started out as an informal but emergency response to the violence slowly grew into something more regular and more important. These meetings created a forum that Des could refer problems to when they arose. He could consult with the leaders or give the point of view of the Christian community, who were a tiny minority in Marawi.

After a while, the group members decided to hold monthly meetings. During this period, Des became close to Aleem Elias Macarandas, who represented the ulama from Marawi, Iligan and Culacao. Both were serious-minded men and greatly respected one another's point of view. Elias felt that Des was very sincere in his efforts; this was exemplified by Des's frequent visits to Elias's house and by the way Des spoke Maranao rather than English, Tagalog or Visayan. Elias also started visiting Des in St Mary's prelature in Iligan and Malabang to discuss the continued unrest.

Both men were concerned that the initial enthusiasm for creating change within the group might be lost. At a meeting on 28 August 1993, Des approached Elias.

'You know Elias, without a formal structure behind these meetings, we might not get anywhere. I know that we are doing some good here, but I'm concerned it might run out of steam unless we have an elected committee who are authorised to make decisions,' Des said in a grave voice, as he looked Elias straight in the eyes.

'You are right,' Elias replied, looking around the room. 'We can't make decisions quickly enough like this. Have you something in mind?'

Des had given this matter some thought and responded immediately. 'We could nominate ten Muslim leaders and ten Christian leaders to meet regularly to continue the movement for peace. We can't ask local people to talk to each other unless the religious leaders are talking to each other too,' Des said.

'Good idea,' Elias responded. 'I'll propose it.'

The proposal was unanimously agreed upon. Although Moctar Matuan didn't consider himself a religious leader, he was elected as one of the ten Muslim leaders as he was the director of the Dansalan Research Center. Professor Maguid Maruhom was also elected to the board as part of the Muslim leadership group. Fr Michel de Gigord (a Paris Foreign Missionary who had been kidnapped twice previously), Fr Nilo Tabania and Fr Rufus Halley were amongst the Christians who participated in the meetings. The committee called itself the Ranau Muslim Christian Movement for Dialogue and Peace.

This was the beginning of sincere and deep friendships between the Muslim and Christian leaders in the area. This group led the way in terms of defining the vision and objectives of the Muslim–Christian dialogue in the area. They were the first in the Philippines to define the kind of relationship that the Muslims and Christians should aspire to.

From this group, there came spin-off groups that were

motivated by the pioneers. One such group was a national forum for bishops, which has since developed into the Bishops–Ulama Conference (BUC). It was established in November 1996 and was part-funded by the government as it was deemed to be part of the peace process. The BUC was made up of twenty-one Mindanao Catholic bishops, twenty-one Muslim ulama and eighteen Protestant bishops. Some of the people in the forum included Archbishop Fernando Capalla, Bishop Hilario Gomez of the Protestant National Council of Churches of the Philippines, and Governor Mahid Mutilan, who represented the Ulama League of the Philippines.

The aim of the BUC was to form a peace dialogue committee and affirm a common commitment and action plan towards building a culture of peace. The BUC has continued to meet and to have quite an influence on the Muslim–Christian dialogue in Mindanao and the wider community ever since. Its formation has been instrumental in bridging Mindanao's socio-cultural and religious divides, and it has made sustained efforts to end the island's many conflicts, most notably the Moro rebellion.

Des felt that the friendships he developed with the Muslim leaders through these committees would prove valuable in stopping the conflict. What he didn't realise, however, was how closely his own life would depend on those friendships in the near future.

CHAPTER 8

If you want peace, work for justice.

Pope Paul VI

When Rufus was living and working in the UK, he took the opportunity to visit his family in Ireland. Unemployment was very high in Ireland during the 1980s and early 1990s. The Halley family ran a law firm Waterford, and his brothers Gerry and Emmet had just taken over their father's practice.

The contrast between the absolute poverty in the Philippines and the affluence of his own family didn't sit well with Rufus. Every time he was home on sabbatical, he remonstrated with his brothers, saying that everyone had too much. During one of these discussions Rufus said to Gerry, 'Why don't you do something? You can afford to employ someone else, even if you don't really need them right now. You don't understand how lucky we are here.'

His words rang true to Gerry, who then spoke to Emmet about what their brother had proposed. They both subsequently agreed to hire someone. A few days later, Emmet told Gerry that he had met a man who had skills they could use in the office. The Halley brothers hired the man and, to their delight, it worked out superbly. He was a great addition to the company and went on to become a permanent member of staff.

Rufus was delighted to hear the news, but while he was always thinking about other people's troubles, his brothers didn't know that at this time he was going through a period of questioning in his personal life. He was thirty-eight years of age and was unsure whether he was following the right path. He had become very friendly with a woman while living in the UK and had started to develop feelings for her. He was so open with his emotions that it was perhaps inevitable he might fall in love with someone.

To work through his feelings, Rufus began to see a therapist named Betty. It wasn't common for men to see therapists at the time, so it was a subject for much conversation among those who knew him.

Word slowly filtered back to the Halley family that he was thinking of leaving the priesthood. His father discussed it with Gerry and voiced his concerns. 'What would people say if he left?' Maxie Halley asked him.

His mother intervened in her usual, understanding way. 'Remember the day he got ordained – you said he'd be welcome home at any time,' Imelda gently reminded him.

'And he would be welcome,' he replied. 'I'd just like to know what's going on.'

To alleviate their father's concerns, Gerry and another brother, Eamonn, decided to visit Rufus to try to find out what his plans were.

Rufus soon heard about the proposed visit, however, and guessing the purpose behind it, he decided to write a letter to Gerry and intervene before they could get to him:

> Might I first say that these questions [the doubts over his path] did not come up because of my being back here studying? I think rather that they were precipitated because of my being back here and my going to see the Analyst. I firmly believe that if I did not face into the storm, the storm would have caught up on me.[1]

He then spoke about when he first realised he needed to see a therapist:

Which then brings me to another point. I don't feel she is a crutch for me (she was for the first number of months) in fact I feel less need of her now.

Rufus told his brother that he was aware of his own weaknesses and that, despite his position in society, he was merely a man. He wrote that he had to decide what to do, and it must be his decision alone:

I must love others, but as much as I love myself. The point being, that I must first be kind to myself. This is all very difficult as I know/[have] been told, how much people look up to me. I'm sorry about that but really they will have to accept that some of their Gods have feet of clay.

His letter continued by apologising for supposedly lying (most likely by omission) to his father about the therapist, but he said he felt his father had enough on his mind without him adding more to it. He finished by making his point in a straightforward but kind tone, leaving the Halley brothers in no doubt that this was a problem they could not help their older brother with:

Boys, your interest and concern are flattering, but please do not be upset if I say that there are some situations better helped by one's absence than one's presence. In fact, the best help that anybody could be to me is by not mentioning the subject at all, at all. I'll tell you though – the odd prayer for my acceptance of God's Will would be great. Thanks to you both. God bless and take care – Ruf.

***

In 1991, Rufus started studying Islamic Studies in the University of Birmingham and was asked to work as a curate in St Jude's church in Maypole, Birmingham, where he stayed until September 1993. Fr Cassidy, the parish priest, was suffering from Parkinson's disease and was unable to cope with the workload. Rufus was more than happy to oblige.

Fr Cassidy's housekeeper, Rosa Allcock, was assigned the task of finding Rufus a place to live. She knew her friend Bridget Hurley, an Irish woman who had emigrated to Birmingham, had a spare room and decided to give her a call.

'Hello Bridget, how are things?'

'Not bad, thanks. What's new with you?'

'I was wondering if you'd like a lodger.'

'What? No thanks.'

'Not even a priest?'

'Well, maybe a bishop, but that's about it,' Bridget replied laughing.

'Well this man is not a bishop, but he is from Ireland.'

Rosa managed to convince her friend, and Rufus soon moved in with her. Any reservations she had about taking in a lodger soon disappeared when she met Rufus for the first time. He greeted her with his customary smile and hug.

'I'm so pleased to meet you,' he said, as he embraced her. 'Thank you so much for letting me stay.'

'It's no problem, you're very welcome,' the Irish woman replied, won over immediately by his warmth, as so many were. They became firm friends, and he soon settled into a routine similar to the one he had kept while living in the Philippines.

Rufus purchased a small scooter and visited the parishioners using his favourite mode of transport. He ate whatever dinner Bridget prepared for him, which usually consisted of potatoes, meat and vegetables – typical Irish food – although Bridget knew he preferred spicy food, so once a week she made a spicy rice dish.

He kept in touch with his family by writing letters, and it was evident from them that he continued to look out for all types of people. He often spoke to his brother Gerry about the problem of growing unemployment in the UK and Ireland. In one of his letters, he asked Gerry to do him a favour, by giving a young barrister a start through the family's legal business. 'I don't know what can be done round the Waterford area – but I feel something should be tried. "You can't run after every hare that rises?" but as the famous writer said, "Nobody ever made a greater mistake than he who did nothing because he thought he could only do a little."' Gerry took Rufus's words to heart, and always made a point of trying to give people a good start in the business when possible.

People who saw this caring trait in Rufus were inspired. John Robinson, who was a lay worker in St Jude's parish, was also called upon to help with Rufus's work. Rufus had been working with a family whose mother was dying of cancer. The three children were in need of help and support, and Rufus assisted in whatever way he could. Before he returned to the Philippines, Rufus asked John to continue to look after the family, especially the children, rather than leaving it to the social workers.[2]

Whenever Rufus came across a situation like this, he always got personally involved and was never afraid to do the right thing. John greatly admired this trait and the two became good friends. While Rufus was based in Birmingham, they went out for dinner a few times. John knew Rufus was not a typical man, and he clearly remembers an occasion when he went to a balti restaurant with Rufus, where a quotation from the Qur'an was written in Arabic on the wall. Rufus astounded the proprietor by reading it and being able to translate it for him.

Perhaps Rufus's greatest gift, however, was his ability to communicate with people in an honest and profound way. His journey of self-discovery, which had begun several years earlier, continued while he was living in Maypole. Although he cared greatly about human suffering and injustice, he was also aware of his personal needs. He understood that he needed to be true to himself. In a letter to his father at the time, he wrote how he couldn't accept money from him, as it would go against his following in Jesus's footsteps:

> I must explain though a bit about not taking any money from you. You know, I almost feel a bit of a 'heel' not taking what you so kindly offer. But my needs are few and one of the things I feel called to do is make my life a little simpler. This vision, if that's what you'd call it, comes from trying to be a follower of a poor man, and also, from the poverty on a grand scale which I've seen in the Philippines. Just rest assured that I will present myself permanently if I have a need.[3]

Rufus's friends have often spoken of his absolute faith in God, and this was apparent in this letter:

> As St Irenaeus once said, 'The Glory of God is in man fully alive.' One of the great sayings I believe. This life which we love so much is God's gift to us – that as Isaiah says, he has carved us in the palm of His hand – and that each of us is always there. But the greatness that each of us is called to is to live out, in imitation of Jesus, every day in the Mass. The total offering of ourselves back to God. My peace is based on the acceptance and living-out of this truth. When God so chooses to accept back this gift which we voluntarily offer, well it is up to him.

Rufus found it effortless to write about his belief and his faith. His father was a very religious man and had been delighted when Rufus decided to become a priest. Rufus enjoyed talking to him about the mystery of faith and their bond deepened over the years through their faith. Whatever country Rufus was in, he wrote letters regularly to his family and friends, and always spoke about the presence of God in his life:

> Thinking of it like this is far from frightening, but rather a new-found freedom and how much greater in every way it is for us to give a gift willingly and cheerfully rather than have it taken off us. When Jesus was on the cross, in ways he was the most helpless of all – yet that was the scene of his triumph, where he could think of others; offer Paradise to the good thief and forgiveness for His torture (forgive them Father) and finally He gave up His Spirit. In other words, he offered back the gift of life to God, and the imitation of which we are all invited to.
>
> With this letter goes my apologies for speaking to my father like this, my Mass today and my love – Rufie.[4]

His friend and classmate, Peter O'Neill, heard rumours around this time that Rufus wasn't going to return to the Philippines at all and that he wanted to spend another year in England. In the end, however, Rufus decided to return after taking some time out to pray and contemplate the decision at a retreat, which turned out to be a deeply religious experience for him and quite transformative.

Another significant factor in influencing his return to the Philippines was undoubtedly the fact that Des, his dear friend, was now the apostolic administrator in Marawi.

In October 1993, Rufus made his way back to Marawi,

stopping on the way in Tunisia, where he went to meet an expert in Muslim–Christian dialogue. He wrote to Celia Eco from there:

> I said goodbye in the parish at the end of August, and also to Betty [his therapist]. It's difficult to say goodbye.
>
> Anyway, after that I went to Belfast to see what they are doing in the area of dialogue. There are so many small groups working there especially on the level of the pastors and the priests. I was very impressed. There is really no substitute to prayer, sharing, joking and eating together – these things are important to do instead of just talking about what to do.

Rufus's work in dialogue was never far from his thoughts and words, and he spoke about the purpose of his trip to Tunisia:

> Anyway, I am here now one week in Tunisia, comparing notes with those who are engaged in dialogue. I'm a bit unlucky because the person I wanted to meet is not here. But the Master will provide for me, we will see. I made my retreat in a Cistercian monastery not so far from my place and something happened that was almost unbelievable. I reaffirmed and reappropriated fully the spiritual dimension of my priesthood, which I have avoided a little over the last 20 years. It was as if I believed myself to be really special and liberal thinking instead of God becoming more important. I believed I was an extraordinary priest, how proud I was. But I also had a chance there to meet with the Charismatics.[5]
>
> Amazing Cel, wait till I tell you. I also asked for help from God because I was feeling depressed sometimes. I knew that God knew what I was feeling and I even

joked with him one time – this morning at the Eucharist, 'Peace be with you', I told God, 'You are hard-headed, I already asked you. Are you deaf? Are you still not doing something for me to put me in order?'

And then when I was at the prayer meeting I asked the Holy Spirit into my life and I surrendered myself to God. All I can say is that I am going in the right direction. I have just re-read this letter and I was thinking that you may think that I am going out of my mind but nothing could be further from the truth. Anyway, I hope to see you on 17 November in Manila.[6]

**

Back in Mindanao, despite the best efforts of the religious leaders, the violence continued to escalate. One evening in August 1994, Des was staying in the Columban house in Cagayan de Oro. He planned on travelling back to Marawi the following morning.

He was an early riser and generally got up about 5.30 a.m., but when he heard the phone ringing at 5 a.m. he knew it could only be bad news. He answered the phone with trepidation.

'Hello?'

Fr Rudi Galenzoga was on the line; he was staying in Des's house in Marawi as he was to host a seminar there the following day.

'Hello, Des. It's Rudi. I'm afraid I have some bad news.'

'Yes, Rudi, what is it?' Des replied, his mind racing with possibilities.

'It's Lydia. She was killed last night. Someone threw a grenade at the house, and she died on her way to the hospital.'

Rudi's voice broke a little while he spoke, and Des sat down because he felt his knees go weak. Lydia Macas had become a good friend. She had looked after the parish newsletter, but her main work was on the radio. Bishop Tudtud had been very keen on using the media as an outlet for promoting the gospel message and even had his own small recording studio in the house. Lydia had regularly recorded a fifteen-minute radio programme, which she then sent into some of the regional Catholic radio stations in the surrounding cities. These stations then broadcast the programmes, which often dealt with issues of the Muslim–Christian dialogue, to a wide audience in Mindanao. This was done in the hope that more and more Christians and Muslims would engage in the dialogue.

'What happened, Rudi?' Des asked in a hoarse voice.

Rudi explained that he had been preparing for bed about 10 p.m. in the seminary building, which is beside the main building, when he heard a huge explosion. The noise was so loud that people heard it in the city centre, about three kilometres away.

As soon as Rudi heard the explosion he ran over to the *convento*, and up the stone steps to where the living area was located. When he entered the living room he saw that a huge hole had been blown in the roof, and that the whole room was covered in rubble and dust. Lydia was still on the chair where she had been sitting watching television, beside another student who had just come over for some media training. Rudi could see that Lydia was badly injured, and her chest and head were bleeding heavily where part of the roof had landed on her.

The other members of the household were just standing there in complete shock. 'Get the car,' Rudi shouted to one of the men, as he lifted Lydia gently and carried her to the car. Her injuries were fatal, however, and she died before they even arrived at the hospital. The girl who had been sitting beside her watching television had somehow been completely unhurt. A Columban sister, Gloria Santos, was also staying in the house that night, but about three minutes before the grenade landed, she had left the *sala* (living room) and gone to her room. She was unharmed, as were the remaining three men who were staying there at the time.

Des rushed back to Marawi and made his way to his house, only to be greeted by a scene of devastation. No one had made any effort to clean it up; they were all too shocked to do anything. The entire living and kitchen area was covered with dust, and most of the ceiling had fallen in. He slowly walked around the room, absorbing the damage, all the while feeling sick in his stomach to think that one of his friends had been murdered in a place that should have been safe. He noticed the holes in the table and the fridge where some of the roof had landed. Some of the debris had come through the wall into his bedroom as well, which was next door to the *sala* area.

Des felt utterly helpless. He knew it would be impossible to find out exactly who was behind the bombing. The members of the household weren't conscious of any enemies, so they couldn't see any reason for the attack. It seemed totally senseless. However, he knew these senseless attacks were happening in the area. Of the seven parish houses in the prelature, five had grenades thrown at them at different times. This left him feeling very vulnerable. One of the biggest questions he had to think about, particularly as he was the apostolic administrator and responsible for the household, was what sort of security precautions he should take. After all, couldn't something like this happen again?

In the following days and weeks, he found it difficult living with the feeling of powerlessness and uncertainty, particularly knowing that the people in government were not going to go to great lengths to find the bombers. That was why he wasn't surprised when no one was brought to justice.

People were afraid to give evidence and remained silent for the sake of survival. To his surprise, Des also found it difficult to speak out about the grenade attack, as he knew that if he made his own enquiries about the bombing he would not only be putting himself in danger, but also those in his household. He wasn't willing to take that risk.

For the next month, the members of the household slept downstairs because they felt protected by the concrete ceiling. They had their evening meal a little earlier for a few weeks, and then everyone would move downstairs by around 7 p.m. Eventually they grew tired of being disrupted, however, and resumed their normal practices and schedules, returning to life as they had known it before. But even that return to normality was not to last long. In Mindanao, violence and mayhem were always on the horizon.

CHAPTER 9

Faithless is he that says farewell when the road darkens.

J. R. R. Tolkien

Lydia's death was covered by the national media and people were horrified to learn that the bishop's house had been bombed. Des's Muslim friends from the Ranau Muslim Christian Movement for Dialogue and Peace came to support him after Lydia's murder. Their response to the bombing taught him that even in a time of crisis, friendships can hold.

This knowledge boosted Des and gave him hope that what they were trying to do was worthwhile, even though it was only on a small scale. Lydia had been very active in the dialogue group and their Muslim friends were upset because they knew the church was trying to live in harmony and dialogue with the Muslim people. They were also aware that this attack provided a negative image of the Muslim people and of the Islamic faith.

Despite the support of his friends, however, Des realised the attack had damaged his trust in people, particularly in people he did not know personally. He started looking over his shoulder and wondering if he was being followed. The bombing made everyone aware that even foreigners and religious orders were now targets, placing them on a par with ordinary Christians, who were frequently attacked.

Des spent a lot of time praying and coming to terms with the attack and murder before he returned to the dialogue meetings. He knew he couldn't preach about dialogue as an ideal while he was suffering from fear and anger. More than ever, he was ultimately forced to acknowledge and accept that while he lived in an Islamic city, he too was vulnerable and was a possible target of attacks in the future.

***

In Malabang, Rufus – who was not long back in the Philippines – was also aware of these dangers, even if he wanted to downplay them. He outlined these issues in a letter to Celia Eco:

> When Paul [Cooney] comes back, I hope to do more, there's not much danger for us here, not even in Marawi, except for the time when one pump boat was robbed last Sunday, where one was shot at.
>
> There is a kidnapping gang around but besides those times I was not afraid, I take care and that's not a problem. At times I feel a little confined. I miss the wide-open spaces of Karomatan but this is where the Master wants me now and I enjoy it also. I don't know enough Maranao, but anyway I am making improvements.[1]

The Paul Cooney mentioned in the letter had been the parish priest in Malabang when Rufus returned to the Philippines, as well as a superior and director of the Columban Missionaries. After a holiday to his home in Co. Cavan in Ireland, however, Cooney returned to Malabang and told Rufus he wanted him to take over his role as parish priest.

While many priests would have been happy to get this position, Rufus declined the offer at first. 'Now, Paul, I'm not being difficult, but we all know that the Christians will manage, but someone has to be there for the Muslims,' Rufus responded. He told Paul this was a big breakthrough for him because he had never wanted to be tied down to anything before; now, however, he wanted to commit to the Muslim people.

Despite Rufus's protestations, Paul ultimately managed to persuade him to take on the role, pointing out that they had very competent staff in the school, Our Lady of Peace High School, which he would have to preside over as part of this new role. In fact, it was more or less running itself, so Rufus would still have a lot of time to pursue his commitment to the Muslim people.

Although Rufus initially found the responsibility a big challenge and very intimidating, he soon realised he really enjoyed it and looked upon it as the best thing that had ever happened to him. He immersed himself completely in the community and, because there were only about 800 Catholic families in his parish, the workload was quite light compared with other parishes. The population of the province, after all, was ninety-seven per cent Muslim.

This lighter workload allowed him to take on other roles and responsibilities, including really immersing himself in his role as the director of Our Lady of Peace High School. This school, built in 1954 by Columban Kenny Koster, catered to both Christian and Muslim children as it was based in part of the Autonomous Region of Muslim Mindanao.[2] It made a big effort to embrace both religions equally, as about half of the 450 pupils were Muslim. The school week ran from Sunday to Thursday, observing the Islamic calendar.

Rufus quickly realised that his role as director of the school was the perfect vehicle for direct access to Maranao families. In general, Muslim society was quite closed and Muslims didn't embrace foreigners easily. Due to his role as director, however, Rufus was able to start visiting the families of the children who had graduated the previous year, and was warmly welcomed into both Christian and Muslim homes. He discovered that once he had visited a Muslim's home their attitude towards him would change, and they became very friendly, and were deeply grateful for the interest he showed in their children.

Rufus made a big effort towards peace and reconciliation within the school and the community. For him, the bedrock of the diocese was the Dialogue of Faith and Life. He strongly believed there must be more than just a 'live and let live' attitude in the long term if there was to be real and lasting change. Therefore, in the school, they celebrated their differences, rather than allowing them to become a source of tension. They celebrated one another's feasts and explored the origin of inter-communal strife and tension. They had Islamic and Catholic teachers in the school, and a prayer room set aside for Muslims.

In 1995, Rufus started renovating the inside of the church. He had a real talent for simplicity, and used bamboo and other locally crafted primary products in the renovation project. Once he was satisfied with how it would look, he handed the project management over to a nun whose taste he admired. This left him more time to engage in dialogue, which was what interested him the most.

Meanwhile, the violence continued around him. In April 1995, two hundred members of Abu Sayyaf attacked a town in Mindanao called Ipil. They raided the banks, shot civilians and torched the centre of the town before taking off again by land and sea.[3] But Rufus refused to let any of the violence affect his behaviour in any way. He continued to visit his parishioners and school children in Malabang in spite of the potential danger to him. He stated often to his friends that he would not be hindered by any threats and he would continue doing the Lord's work, no matter what dangers he faced.

***

Venus Guibone, a longtime friend of Rufus, was working as a lay worker in a Columban parish in Sinacaban. Rufus had some free time and decided to pay her a surprise visit. When he arrived, however, he discovered that she was two towns away in Panaon, facilitating a graduating retreat for high school students. Even though she was working and he had never been to Panaon, he decided to continue his journey and find her.

Venus was in the middle of talking to the students when she saw him walking outside the window. She thought she had seen a ghost.

'My God,' she exclaimed, and then gave the students something to read while she went out to him. 'I can't believe it, Popong,' she declared, using his Filipino name. 'I had no idea you were around,' she said, throwing her arms around him.

'I wasn't around,' he responded with a grin. 'I came to see you.'

Venus was a practical person by nature, so although she was delighted to see her friend, she was also conscious of her commitments to the students.

'Gosh, I still have one more session tomorrow and I'm not finished for today either, so we won't have much time to talk,' she said dejectedly.

Rufus smiled. 'Don't worry, Venus. We do have time. Sure, I'll stay overnight, so we'll have plenty of time.'

He spent the night at the nearby parish rectory with Fr Pat Steen, who was then the parish priest. Fr Steen invited Venus to join them for supper and she discovered Popong had brought ice cream wrapped in newspaper, which they ate for dessert.

After supper, Popong walked with Venus to the sisters' convent nearby and after she had introduced him to the sisters they had a good long chat.

Venus wasn't very much into writing letters, so whenever Rufus would visit her their chats were always long and intimate; this was something she always looked forward to. Popong was naturally loving, thoughtful and loyal to his family and friends. Each time he visited Venus he would always have a *pasalubong* (Filipino for something a friend or guest would bring for the one they visited), which could be ice cream, chocolates, flowers or candies. Venus saw in this meeting how Rufus's psychoanalysis had made him even freer.

That evening, she asked him to help at the retreat the following morning. Normally when she organised events or talks, she would ask someone weeks in advance to speak at it, but she knew Rufus was spontaneous by nature, so would enjoy contributing at short notice.

'What is it about?' he asked.

'This would be perfect for you,' Venus said. 'It's about availability.'

'Oh, why not,' Rufus agreed with a smile.

The following morning, when she introduced him to the students, she said that he was 'the epitome of availability'. She spoke from the deepest recesses of her heart.

'You are just so lucky. There is somebody here who is just perfect for this particular topic. You are not just lucky; you are blessed. And he is not just a friend, but really somebody who has always been available. Please enjoy.'

Rufus stood in front of the class, holding out some rice stalks for them to see.

'I stole some rice stalks from the rice fields,' he said. 'I come from a country that has wheat.' He went on to talk about the parable of the grain of wheat that is in the New Testament of the Bible. 'Until a grain of wheat falls to the ground and dies, it remains a single grain of wheat, but if it dies it yields much fruit.'[4]

Venus sat back, wondering what this had to do with the topic of availability.

He used the rice stalk as a prop, and completely engaged the students saying, 'This is what Jesus meant. The field out there is the fruit of these seeds, seeds that had to die in order to grow. This is what Jesus did for us. He died for us, just like the wheat, or this rice, so that we may live. He lives in us. He became available to the point of death.'

He said all this in Cebuano, with a little English, as these were fourth-year high school students. Venus watched and saw how the students were captivated by this white man who spoke from the heart in their own language.

After the workshop, she told him she was worried about him, given the escalation of violence in the region. 'I don't know, Rufus, but I've always prayed for your safety. I'm always afraid that something is going to happen to you.'

'Well, thanks be to God, Venus, I'm still alive.'

'I really thank God for you,' she said and started to sing. '"I thank my God each time I think of you, and when I pray for you, I pray with joy." It's a song taken from St Paul's letter to the Philippians.'

'Gosh, I'm flattered,' Rufus replied, slightly taken aback.

'I mean that, I really mean that,' Venus said emotionally as she reached out and held his hand.

***

The inter-faith meetings in Mindanao continued to go from strength to strength, and when Fr Paul Glynn moved to Sultan Naga Dimaporo in 1996, he soon became involved. The first time he attended a meeting, both Des and Rufus were present, as were two other Irish priests, Kevin McHugh and Dave Cribbin, as well as Ben Maes from Belgium.

Des needed someone to take on the role of coordinator between the Muslims and the Christians. After a few minutes, someone proposed that Rufus should do this because he was good at the language and he could communicate effectively with people.

Rufus leaned forward and clasped his hands. 'You know what? I think Des should do it. Des, you're very good at organising things.'

Des couldn't contain his exasperation. 'For God's sake, Hals! I've too much to do, that's why I'm asking someone else to take over.'

Rufus hated administrative work, and he also hated being tied down to more commitments, but he wanted to help as much as he could, so he reluctantly agreed to this new task.

During these meetings, Paul saw that Rufus was a man who wanted to be transparent. He was someone who was self-aware and knew his strengths and weaknesses. He appeared very light-hearted and always approachable, and he was able to laugh at himself and his mistakes. What you saw was what you got.

At one meeting, a priest asked Rufus about Muslim–Christian dialogue and looked for advice on the best way to handle it. Paul was fascinated by his answer.

Rufus said, 'You must first learn to dialogue with yourself. We all have a good side and a shadow side. You must learn how to talk to the little demons that are inside you; otherwise you'll never be able to talk – and to listen – to others. Once you have started your internal dialogue, however, then you can start talking to other people.'

What Rufus was saying was that there was no point in having good relations with Muslims if you were fighting with other Columbans, which Rufus had been known to do over the years. He once confided in Paul that he was embarrassed about some of the things he had done when he first arrived in the Philippines. 'You know, when I look back at how I acted in Jala-Jala, I cringe.

I should have been more thoughtful to the priests that were there ahead of me. I just went ahead and did it my way without giving any thought to them.'

Paul was so impressed by his ability to be humble. He wasn't afraid to admit when he was wrong. Rufus threw himself into the meetings and was working well in his new capacity, until in March 1996 he had to go home to Waterford suddenly, because he got news that his father was very ill.

While there, Rufus continued to document his thoughts. He wrote to Celia about his father, saying:

> I knew that I was very proud of him, partly perhaps because I was no longer envious of him. Perhaps that results from my feeling that I can rival him in my own way, by wholeheartedly accepting the responsibility of parish priest and director of the school of Malabang. Yes, I have so much to thank God for because he is always caring towards me. As for us, that we be free and open to go where he wants and to do what God wants, that's how he really helps us to grow.
>
> Anyway, after two hours driving we arrive home and it was a very tender and emotional reunion with my father. God is good. And I had a marvellous two days with him. We spoke about death and he was even able to have a mystical experience of God a few months ago which he shared with me, then he went to confession with me and we had a great Eucharist together with many of the growing children around too. He was also joking so I was ready then when on the Sunday afternoon he had a stroke.[5]

His father subsequently passed away on 8 April and Rufus soon returned to his parish in Malabang. He continued to work quietly and steadily with the Muslims and Christians. Though the random attacks and violence continued to take place, slowing the process even more, Rufus engaged in the process enthusiastically in the strong belief that he was doing God's work. But, all the while, he could see how the tension was growing between the MNLF and the government. In a letter to Celia in August, he wrote about his fears of a further escalation of violence:

> The MNLF have compromised already and if they are not accepted, there will really be a war, which we must avoid above all.[6]

And, sure enough, the consequences of these tensions were about to crash down upon the Columbans, and on one priest in particular.

II

THE ABDUCTION

CHAPTER 10

I know God will not give me anything I can't handle.
I just wish that He didn't trust me so much.

Mother Teresa

Commander Lakay Macabunta and his wife, Laon, were nervous as they knocked on Des's door. As Lakay was a commander in the MNLF, they should have felt secure in Marawi, but they were about to betray a friend, so their palms were covered with a thin layer of sweat.

It didn't sit comfortably with them. Des had always been generous with his time and had even given them money when they needed a doctor for their children. Whatever they had requested in the past, Des had not refused; this was the very reason they were the ones chosen to go to him with this 'request'.

He greeted the couple as friends, as he always did. 'Lakay, Laon! How is your family? Is everything okay?'

'Yes, Padre, thank you,' Lakay said. 'But we need your help with something. I am in trouble with my people. Some of them think I have received the money that was promised from the government and have kept it to myself. I have set up a meeting in Iligan next week to explain to them that the government has broken its promise. Fr Rufil will come to show that what I say is true. If you come along, too, it will give much greater credibility to me.'

The church in Iligan had recently become involved in negotiating the details of the MNLF's surrender to the government, with Archbishop Fernando Capalla even helping to work out the particulars between the two warring sides. Des had always been uneasy with this relationship. He didn't think the church's role was to be a liaison between the government and the rebels, and thought it put the church in a position of power. The fact that the Iligan church was to be used as a conduit for the money from the government to the rebels made him particularly nervous. But Fr Rufil Quibranza, who was involved in the negotiations, was a local Corpus Christi priest whom he trusted, and Des felt a strong impulse to support him in this situation.

Lakay feared that Des would not get involved in this negotiation, especially as the priest knew little about the particulars of the situation, and he knew that Des never rushed any decision. Des was well known among his colleagues and friends for taking his time to mull over matters. He contemplated and prayed over all major decisions. But Lakay also knew of Des's innate sense of goodness and justice, and sensed that he could appeal to him in this way.

The Irish priest reacted in a predictable fashion.

'But I have nothing to do with it. Fr Rufil is the one ...'

'Yes,' Lakay interrupted. 'Fr Rufil knows about it, and he knows that I didn't get the money. But if you were there it would have much greater credibility with my people,' he repeated.

Des sighed heavily as he contemplated what the commander was asking of him. His opinion was that the negotiations should have been done through government offices. However, despite his reservations about the negotiations, he never suspected that Lakay might be leading him into a trap.

He looked at the face of Lakay's wife and thought she looked stressed and under pressure. In the evening shadows she appeared almost child-like, although her face was drawn and tense. The only thing that gave her age away was her faint stoop, as if she was buckling underneath the burdens she was carrying.

He suddenly made up his mind, which was unlike him. The

fact that Iligan wasn't regarded as a dangerous area helped him decide so promptly. He also knew that Archbishop Capalla wanted to see the negotiation through and was involved in further dialogue to see that this happened. In addition, of course, he wanted to help Lakay, whom he regarded as a close acquaintance. He did hesitate again when he remembered he had to give a talk in Pagadian in a few days. But, after another moment's thought, he figured he could still make Lakay's meeting afterwards. He really wasn't too keen at being involved at that level, but he wanted to help.

'Okay, I'll come along. It's not a big deal. If it helps you out and if Rufil has the details of what was given and what wasn't given, I'm ready to go along.'

The commander and his wife thanked him, relieved.

***

When Des finished his talk in Pagadian, he went to the Columban house in Ozamiz to relax for the evening and catch up with his friends and colleagues. He slept dreamlessly that night, as was usual for him.

The next day he caught the early morning boat across the bay to the priest's house at the rectory in Kolambugan, where he had arranged to meet Fr Rufil Quibranza. He had planned his day carefully: he was going to travel back to Iligan with Rufil once the meeting concluded, where he would be picked up and brought back to Marawi.

Rufil got into his white Suzuki jeep, and Des hopped into the passenger seat beside him, throwing his small backpack at his feet. He had a habit of travelling with some essentials as he would often be delayed on assignments and was never quite sure when he would make it back home. On this occasion, as well as a change of clothes and toiletries, he also had a small breviary, a short-wave radio and an Agatha Christie novel called *Towards Zero*. He always packed several T-shirts, because although he had left his home in Ireland many years previously, he still found the heat in the Philippines almost unbearable and often needed to change his top several times throughout the day.

The jeep made little noise in the early morning light as it drove along the dirt track towards the beach in Kolambugan. When they arrived on the beach, some of Lakay's colleagues from the MNLF were already present. Des asked if they were almost ready to proceed but was told that not all of them could attend the meeting in Kolambugan, so it had been moved to Saginsagin, in a school above the town. The fact that the school was situated beyond the military checkpoints on the way to the mountain didn't seem suspicious to either Des or Rufil.

Lakay and Laon jumped into the back of the jeep behind the two priests and Rufil drove slowly and carefully up the track, concentrating on staying on the road. Des trained his eyes to the left, noticing that there was only one wooden house situated on the rocky terrain. The Irish man was at ease with his Filipino companions, and for the most part they drove in a comfortable silence, although occasionally they conversed in Maranao. Des was tired after his trip to Pagadian and was looking forward to going home.

Out of nowhere a jeepney appeared behind them. *Beep beep beep*!

At the same time, a voice behind them shouted, 'Stop, stop!'

Commander Lakay shouted that they'd gone past the arranged meeting spot, so Rufil slowly reversed his jeep into the bushes and was about to turn around when two things happened simultaneously.

About ten armed men exited the jeepney behind them and surrounded their vehicle. Des saw one of them lean in and take the keys out while Rufil felt the unmistakable tip of a .45 calibre gun being pressed against his left temple.

Des and Rufil both realised at the same time that they had been kidnapped. Des immediately made the connection to his so-called friends. *We've been betrayed; we've been taken! We've been kidnapped*, he thought silently.

As the two men sat there, feeling dazed, their abductors manhandled them out of the white Suzuki jeep and into the jeepney, which was still parked behind them, blocking the road.

Des quickly thought of his travel bag.

'I want my bag, the bag is important.'

'Oh, the bag, the bag of Fr Des – get it!' one of the older kidnappers instructed.

One of the young men transferred the bag into the jeepney, while another jumped into Rufil's jeep and completed the manoeuvre the priest had started. Des and Rufil sat opposite each other in the back of a blue Armac passenger jeepney, surrounded by their kidnappers.

They covered most of the priests' heads with a malong. One of the men insisted on also lowering the heavy plastic flaps at the side of the jeepney, to obscure the vision in and out of the vehicle. These were normally only used in the rain, but Des correctly surmised that their intention was to hide the priests' identities if they passed the military at any point.

Des, who had been sitting there in a type of daze, came to his senses and started admonishing Lakay. He said that Lakay had betrayed him in the strongest sense of the word. In the Maranao dialect, the word has an even stronger resonance than in English.

'You are a traitor, Lakay. You have betrayed us both.'

Lakay looked very embarrassed. He didn't reply, but his silence spoke volumes to the priest. His wife, who was sitting beside him, just turned her head away from Des.

Then Des became conscious of a man beside him who had a handcuff on his right hand. This man attempted to put the other cuff onto the priest's hand, but Des reacted instinctively and pulled his hand away.

'You're not dealing with a criminal.'

'*Calma*, take it easy,' the man responded.

Despite his dangerous situation, Des was trying to assert a certain authority. The fact that there were ten armed men pointing guns at him meant his choices were limited, of course, but he was determined to keep up some semblance of authority and human dignity in what was rapidly turning into a nightmarish situation.

Des looked at the men beside him and realised this was not an amateur operation. Several of the men in his company were likely senior MNLF commanders, and the fact that they called one of the men the 'Black Panther' indicated to Des that he was seated with the top echelons of the rebels. He quietly observed that they called the man beside him 'Mamaki' and that none of them had made any attempt to disguise their identities. Des took this as a grim sign.

Rufil also sat in complete shock and silence. He had taken over the negotiations when Archbishop Capalla was transferred to Davao, but he had never in his wildest dreams imagined it might lead to him being taken captive one day. After all, he had worked tirelessly on behalf of the rebel returnees – those who had negotiated with the government and accepted their terms – to ensure they received the money promised by the government. He simply could not comprehend why they would betray him in this manner.

Des noticed that Rufil had lost his colour and looked faint. He was clearly in shock. Des leaned towards him and put his hand on his shoulder.

'Okay, Rufil, don't worry. We will get out of this.'

Rufil didn't reply. He merely concentrated on breathing, feeling his shallow breath fight against the humid air.

Des noticed they had started travelling uphill, into the mountains. The road was very rugged and slippery and, had they continued on this route, they would have come to a small mountain town called Tangcal. The abductors were afraid to go into the town, however, for fear of being seen, so when they were about five or ten kilometres away the jeepney pulled into a cornfield.

Lakay nudged Des, indicating he should disembark.

'Come on, Padre. We must walk from here.'

The party walked about half a kilometre through the fields until they reached a two-storey wooden house, which appeared like a vision through the yellow corn. Here they were met by teenage boys holding .45 and .38 calibre guns. Despite the searing heat, Des gave an involuntary shudder at the sight of them, as he realised these boys had been given no choice in the destiny they were handed. Lakay and Laon went into the house, but Des and Rufil were told to wait outside with the younger guards until the commanders arrived.

Rufil's fear, which had kept him silent until that point, suddenly found its voice. 'Are you going to hurt us? Are you going to kill us?'

He became more boisterous with every question and Des, taking charge of the situation, put his hand on Rufil's shoulders and said in a low voice, 'Stop complaining, Rufil. These men are nervous. Stop complaining now.'

Rufil complied, giving Des the chance to speak to their captors.

'You know we are relatives of Demacori's?'

Rufil was related to a congressman, Demacori, who was a very powerful figure in the Philippines. Des wasn't related, of course, but by saying 'we' he was associating himself with the Demacoris, a dynasty most rebels would have been afraid to cross. The guards, however, told them they were already aware of this.

'Take it easy,' one of the guards said. 'We won't kill you because you are the cousin of Demacori. We only want you to deliver a message.'

This gave Rufil some courage, so he spoke up again. 'I've been helping you for eighteen years, working with you all this time,' he exclaimed. 'Why are you doing this to me?'

'President Ramos has forgotten us. We have to get you because you are known, so maybe the president will listen today.'

The two priests shook their heads but knew that there was nothing for them to do but wait and see what would happen next.

As the sun rose high in the sky, nearing midday, Lakay called the priests into the house and offered them lunch.

***

They spent the next few hours in the house, waiting. Des remained sitting, contemplating the situation and trying to preserve his energy, as he was conscious it would be a long day. Meanwhile, Rufil paced back and forth nervously, lost in his own thoughts and convinced he would never make it back to the city alive. Des was conscious that his fellow priest had become a little overwhelmed by the situation, so he continued to comfort him.

'We'll get through this, we'll be okay.'

He felt quite strong; he believed he would be able to cope with whatever happened. He felt a power within him, and believed that what he felt wasn't his own. This strength came from his belief in a higher source.

The captors had an animated discussion in the next room.

Afterwards, the priests discovered that the rebels had decided they were going to bring Rufil back to the city to take part in the negotiations. However, they would take Des into the mountains.

Rufil's knees buckled in relief, although he looked stricken at the thought of Des remaining captive. But Des felt quite calm and peaceful; if anything, he was surprised he didn't feel any fear in that particular moment. 'I'll be okay, Rufil. I feel okay.' He realised that being a Westerner, he was the more valuable hostage, so really it had come as no surprise to him that they refused to release him.

Lakay's wife, Laon, was charged with taking Rufil back to Kolambugan. Just as the two groups were about to separate, she came over to shake the Irish priest's hand.

Des froze as she held out her hand, looked at her and walked away. He wasn't ready to shake hands with a person who had betrayed him. The priest was a man of God, but he was also a man with human emotions, after all. He was never able for any pretence in relationships. The guards all noticed what had happened. Des later said that he had not intended to embarrass Laon publicly; it was just that he was not ready to be reconciled because it was just hours since he had been betrayed. He could see that Lakay was also embarrassed, but he didn't say anything.

Reconciliation is very difficult in Maranao culture and it seldom happens without much negotiation and after a lot of bloodshed. Maranaos always feel they have to take revenge when they are wronged. Des felt, therefore, that the guards understood his position.

The MNLF dropped Rufil back to his jeep in Kolambugan, giving him a sheet of paper with a list of demands that he was to pass to the government. Before he drove away, they asked what food the foreign priest would eat. Rufil replied that he ate rice and fruit, like them.

Back in the mountains beside Tangcal, the kidnappers tried to reassure Des that he would come to no harm. They told him their argument was with the government.

'You are not being kidnapped; you are being taken as a hostage.'[1]

As if he had any doubt as to his status; after all, he was surrounded by ten heavily armed guards, who had Armalites, grenades and sub-machine guns. They carried side arms as well as .45 calibre guns; many of them wore belts of bullets across their chests. They were quite fearsome to look at.

'Come on, Padre,' one of the older guards said to Des, in a kindly tone. 'Let's go. We have a long way to walk.'

Des said a small prayer of thanks as he was led from the house. At least he was wearing his sturdy shoes, instead of the sandals he usually wore. They would surely help as he set off on a journey, the length and destination of which he knew nothing about.

CHAPTER 11

No matter how steep the mountain –
the Lord is going to climb it with you.

Helen Steiner Rice

Fr Rufil quickly drove back to his parish of Iligan, where he called Monsignor Leo, his superior in Corpus Christi. He briefly outlined what had happened. Leo immediately called Bishop Bataclan, the bishop of Iligan, setting in motion a chain of events that he hoped would lead to Des's release.

Bataclan realised that Archbishop Capalla also needed to know what had taken place. Once informed, Capalla was both decisive and swift in assuming authority. He immediately rang President Fidel Ramos and told him the list of demands that had been given to Rufil by the kidnappers. Capalla also implored the president not to attempt a rescue operation, as he was afraid of putting Des's life in danger. The president agreed that a rescue attempt would be a bad idea at this stage, and he agreed to meet with the heads of the church to discuss the situation.

The archbishop could see why the priest had been taken hostage. After several years of negotiations between the Philippine government and the MNLF, the 1996 Final Peace Agreement had been signed on 2 September. As part of the agreement, the government was supposed to give the MNLF funding for their livelihood projects, as well as for the other items on the list of demands. When this didn't happen, the MNLF went to the governmental offices in Manila and stated their demands. However, the money for their livelihood projects, totalling thirteen million pesos, was still outstanding over a year later. Des was now, it seemed, a pawn in these negotiations.

In the meantime, Rufil hid in his room, severely traumatised by the incident. Capalla instructed him not to talk to the media or reveal the kidnapping to the general public; he was afraid it would interfere with the negotiations between the government and the MNLF rebels.

Rufil was terrified, and jumped every time the phone rang. He couldn't understand why his friends had betrayed him. At the same time, as he sat in his room, he mulled over the demands the MNLF had made. The demands included the immediate release of all livelihood project claims already processed by the National Program for Unification and Development Council (NPUDC); the provision of farming-related services through the Department of Agriculture; scholarship grants; skills training; primary healthcare; legal assistance; and basic infrastructure.[1] Rufil found himself getting angry with the president as he dwelt on these demands. He realised the government had broken their promise to the rebels. If they'd kept their word, Des wouldn't be in the awful situation he currently found himself in.

***

At first, Des didn't know what his abductors' demands were. The only thing his guards told him was that he was not being kidnapped; he was being taken as a hostage and that their argument was with the government. He was aware the peace negotiations had taken years to come to any type of fruition, and he was unsure, therefore, how long it would take the government to react to this particular situation. Later, when he heard them say something about thirteen million pesos, he feared he would be held for a long, long time.

He continued walking along the trail, which was on a plateau. There was a high mountain to the left and a valley with rolling lush land on his right. He was surprised to meet several people on the route as he had expected the guards to keep his whereabouts a secret. One woman they met asked who he was, and the rebels told her Des was the second-in-command to James Bond. This struck Des as odd, as he didn't expect the woman to be well-versed in Western pop culture. He later found out that one of the commanders was known as James Bond.

After about thirty minutes of walking on the flat, they turned towards the mountain and started walking uphill. The terrain was quite difficult and they took many breaks. Des often got tired and said, 'I'm sitting down.'

His guards were quite anxious, however, because they were afraid the army would come to rescue him, so his breaks never lasted long.

They walked for about two hours non-stop in the humid, muggy air, going higher up the mountain. Eventually, at about 3.30 p.m., they levelled off onto another plateau area and came across a small, derelict house. The young guard who had accompanied Des along the trail said, 'We're going to stay here for the night.'

Once inside the house, Des saw that there was just a kitchen, a *sala* area and one bedroom. The guards put Des in the bedroom and told him he could rest. The bed consisted of a few wooden planks in the corner. Des sat down, allowing his body to recuperate from the steep climb. A few minutes later his guard came in and said, 'Don't be afraid, there's going to be shooting. Batman, the sharpshooter, is trying to shoot a bird.'

Des went outside to see what was happening and covered his ears with his hands as he saw Batman raise the rifle in the air. The bird was sitting on a tree about twenty metres away, and the bullet hit it perfectly in the neck. Any thoughts Des had of escaping disappeared in that minute.

The guards prepared the bird and ate it with some rice. It seemed to Des that they were almost unprepared for his kidnapping, as they had very few provisions with them. All they had brought was rice. Des told them he needed boiled water to drink.

'If you don't boil the water for me and if my stomach gets upset because of the water, or if I get diarrhoea, you'll have a dead hostage and that's no good to you,' Des told them that first night. 'You will be the ones with your lives on the line if anything happens to me,' he warned.

He fell asleep easily that night and, to his surprise, slept quite well. The roofing was solid, with wooden slats overlying each other, and it protected him from the heavy rain that fell.

The next morning they had plain rice for breakfast, left over from the previous night's dinner. Des took the opportunity to talk to his guards and to try to start relating to them. He asked them something that had been on his mind.

'Why didn't you let me go and keep Fr Rufil?'

They answered him in Visayan, '*Ikaw ang dako*', which meant, 'You are the heavy one/you're the heavyweight.'

He understood that the government would come under more pressure to resolve his situation because he was a foreigner. Any time a Filipino priest had been kidnapped within the Philippines, it didn't make international news.

He had to remain in the house for the day, but he did have a number of things in his bag that proved useful. As well as his breviary, novel and a spiritual reading book, he had some yellow notepaper in his bag and a pen, so he started keeping a diary of what was happening. That day he wrote a short note about what he had learned from the guards:

Tuesday, 28th October 1997

My captors told me they are demanding 13 million pesos from the government. In my bag I have my little breviary and little radio. The local Ozamiz radio said nothing about me.

He picked up his breviary, lay back on his planks and began to read. The day passed slowly.

***

Fr Donie Hogan was the superior in charge of the Columbans in the Philippines at the time, so it was he who first received a phone call about the kidnapping from Archbishop Capalla. Donie, from Waterford in Ireland, was good friends with Des. He felt sick when Capalla told him what had happened. Capalla explained that the rebels were using Des as leverage to have their demands met. Donie knew he had to stop the military getting involved at all costs; it would lead to bloodshed if they attempted to rescue Des, and his main priority was to keep Des safe. He immediately began working through all political and diplomatic channels to ensure the safety and speedy release of Des.

Fr Evergisto Bernaldez was working in Karomatan when a man from the parish told him Des had been kidnapped. Although he was somewhat shocked to hear the news, he was always waiting for bad news such as this, because there was such a history of violence in the area. There was always some expectation among the religious orders that it could happen. And now it had.

Evergisto left Karomatan immediately and went to Marawi to offer support to Des's colleagues. Fr Chito Yanoc, who had been in charge of the media ministry since Lydia's murder, was in the bishop's house. Both men immediately started contacting Des's closest Muslim friends, including Aleem Elias Macarandas and Sultan Moctar Matuan, in order to look for support. They knew that Des trusted these men deeply.

Elias had just returned from Egypt when he received a phone call from Evergisto, telling him his friends had kidnapped Des. He could tell that Evergisto was upset and angry. Elias knew the people who had taken Des were former MNLF commanders who had been let down by the government. While he was sympathetic to the commanders and their predicament, he knew it wasn't right to use Des as a pawn in the negotiations. As soon as he heard the news, he travelled to Kolambugan in Lanao del Norte.

Elias was related to one of the kidnappers, so he got in touch with him immediately. He told him to take good care of Des and to make sure he wasn't harmed. At 9.30 a.m. the following day he went to Tangcal to Commander Tigre at Beneslan.

'Why have you kidnapped this foreign priest who has been working so hard with the Muslim people?' he asked Commander Tigre.

'The government has not kept their side of the agreement,' Tigre answered agitatedly. 'They don't listen to us. We have been trying to meet with them for months, but it makes no difference. This is the only way they will take us seriously.'

Elias stayed silent as he knew there was truth in what Tigre said. He reminded him once again to keep Des safe, and then returned home.

Another man with whom Des had become friends while learning Maranao, Maguid Maruhom, read about Des's kidnapping in the newspaper. He felt helpless and prayed for him night after night. He found it hard to accept that his friend had been taken by the MNLF, as he knew it reflected badly on all Muslims. Through his own network of friends, he learned that the background to the kidnapping was political and he was relieved to hear that the Muslim community was treating Des well and fairly.

***

Des was having a quieter time than he'd initially expected. He read a lot and was amazed to find that he wasn't really afraid; in fact, he was quite relaxed. He knew he had been brought to the region of Lanao del Norte and this surprised him, as he was aware that Lakay was part of the MNLF, which was based in Lanao del Sur. He didn't know he had been handed over to a Lanao del Norte-based group within the MNLF for logistical reasons. The MNLF members from Lanao del Sur felt they didn't have everything in place to keep him safely.

On his second day up the mountain, a small number of his kidnappers went down to Kolambugan to get supplies and to see what was happening with the negotiations. Des waited for them the whole day, but they didn't return. At about 8 p.m. that night he went to sleep, but shortly after dozing off, there was a commotion. The group had returned, and they told him, 'We have to move out immediately.'

They had heard that the army had mobilised and was going to come in from the other side of the mountain. The kidnappers packed up everything and moved further into the forest. It was extremely difficult, because it had been raining and the night was so dark that Des could not see his feet in front of him.

One of the men took Des's arm and guided him through the forest as he slipped and slid along. After walking for roughly thirty minutes they came to a small clearing and one of the men said, 'We're going to stay here.'

'Where?' Des asked.

'Here!'

Des looked around him and his heart sank as he realised he would be staying out in the open forest that night. They threw planks of wood on the ground and a young guard cut a few branches off a tree and put them over the planks as a kind of shelter.

'That's where you're going to sleep.'

He noticed the ground wasn't level, and wondered if there were snakes or animals around. He looked towards the sky and noticed how brightly the thousands of stars shone. When he lay back into his makeshift tent – or cell, he forlornly thought – he could see the sky through the branches, and watched the stars glinting and glowing in the thick darkness. It reminded him of Yahweh's promise to Abraham (Genesis 26:4): 'Your descendants will become as numerous as the stars of the sky.' Although Des was very uncomfortable on the planks, he wondered how the guards managed to sleep at all, as they were forced to simply lie on the wet ground.

Despite everything, he slept quite well that night, until the rain came at about 3 a.m. The noise of the raindrops on the leaves woke him. He couldn't believe how the few branches protected him from the worst of the rain; he lay and watched the water turn into little rivulets and fall to the ground beyond his shelter.

At 5 a.m. the guards rose, lit a fire and cooked a breakfast of rice, canned sardines and coffee. As soon as breakfast was over, they said, 'We're moving again.' Everyone quickly moved down the mountain. Des was surprised by the direction they were heading. Three guards walked ahead as an advance party, then Des followed with one or two men by his side and another three or four at the back.

At the bottom of the mountain, they stopped at a house on a plateau area. Des asked if he could wash and shave. He had his bathing trunks and toothbrush in his bag. The guards agreed to his request and two of them accompanied him to the river, carrying their Armalites casually over their shoulders. He refreshed himself by splashing around the shallow waters. When he got back to the house, he enjoyed a nice meal of chicken cooked in coconut milk.

Later that afternoon, the rebel returnees of the MNLF turned him over to the ex-mayor of Tangcal, the kingpin of the Tangcal region, who was referred to as the *forda* (head guard). The transfer happened about twenty kilometres from the town, in a very remote area. The returnees were concerned that someone would alert the army to Des's presence while they were holding him, but they felt the ex-mayor had complete control over the people in his area, so there'd be no fear of Des's whereabouts becoming known if the priest was held by him. The kingpin was a former Maranao captain and always wore a balaclava in front of Des.

After a brief meal following the exchange, his new guards told him they had to move. Des noticed how they didn't have a problem moving him around in broad daylight, although this was to change later in his captivity as the guards became more anxious.

They soon reached cornfields, where the corn was about six or seven feet tall. Nobody could see them in there. There was a hut in the middle of the fields and Des was informed that they planned to stay there for a while. One of his guards, Juan, who it later turned out was the ex-mayor's eldest son, went in to clean it up but ran out immediately surrounded by a swarm of bees. Seeing how badly he had been stung, they decided to leave the hut to the bees and moved on. At the outskirts of the village they met a few people, including a man on a carabao, a domestic water buffalo native to the Philippines.

'If you say anything or if you tell anyone that you've met us, you'll have your throat slit,' one of the guards warned him.

At about 3 p.m. they came to a house where the family invited the group in. From the warm welcome they received, Des thought they were related to the guards. They had prepared a meal of chicken and rice and gave Des a space to rest. As dusk approached, the man of the house prepared to pray, and Des took the opportunity to read his evening prayer in his breviary. While he was reading there was an alert and the guards said, 'We have to move, we have to move!'

Through his experience of dealing with Muslims Des knew how important prayer was to them and that once they begin to pray, they continue until they are finished. He guessed it wasn't a big emergency, and he wanted to make the point that Christians are also people of prayer and their prayers should not be interrupted.

'No, I have to finish my prayer,' he said.

They gave him the space and time he requested and he continued reading until he was finished. Only then did he pack up.

They went back towards the village, which was in the centre of the area controlled by the ex-mayor. After skirting the village a few times, they brought him into the village centre. Des took it as a good sign that they were so open and relaxed with the villagers.

Des sat in a little shop and the proprietor gave him a glass of Coke and bread. He enjoyed the cool darkness of the shop. Many of the children and women in the village came in just to have a look at him, as it was very seldom a white foreigner came into their area.

One of the guards told the villagers, 'We're only here to rest for a while and then once it gets dark we're going to take a ten-hour hike into Lanao del Sur.' Des was quite apprehensive when he heard this. He was already tired; he didn't relish the thought of a long trek and was genuinely concerned he might not survive it.

He was hugely relieved when he discovered this was a lie. Instead they merely walked along the trail outside the village for about ten minutes and then turned into a densely forested area. They continued walking until they came to a little hut his captors had prepared for him. The first thing Des noticed about this location was how savage the mosquitoes were. On the high mountain there had been no mosquitoes at all.

Des said, 'I have to have a mosquito net. I won't survive without a mosquito net.'

'Oh yes,' Juan said, 'we'll get it tomorrow.'

'No, you'll get it now,' Des asserted, although they were about a forty-minute walk from the village.

'No,' Juan said, 'I'll get it tomorrow.'

'No! Go back and get it now or I'll have malaria by the morning.'

Juan sullenly gave in to Des's demands and reluctantly returned to the village. Although the rebels had taken away his basic freedom, Des wanted to at least attempt to preserve a level of dignity below which he would refuse to go. He understood their demands and that he was a hostage in order to bargain with the government, but he was determined he wouldn't allow them to dehumanise him. It helped that the guards were trying to stay friendly with him and keep him happy and alive. He felt a mosquito net in these circumstances was a relatively normal request; after all, it was important to keep him healthy. Admittedly, he wanted it more for his own comfort than for combating the threat of malaria, but there was no harm in being extra cautious.

The hut was about six feet by eight feet, and was well concealed about twenty metres above a river. There was a little elevated space for him and the guards slept on planks below him. It was comfortable when it didn't rain, but when it rained the water seeped down the mountain into the bed space. Des could hear the river flowing all night.

At about 5 a.m. Juan pulled up the mosquito net and said, 'Have you got malaria yet?'

Des just laughed. He tried to retain a sense of humour, to not let his negative feelings overwhelm him.

He was to struggle with this negativity during the entire time of his captivity: he felt deep resentment at being taken captive and the fact that it had been his friends who had betrayed him. These feelings threatened to overwhelm him at times, and he had to pray hard to find strength from the word of God.

CHAPTER 12

If you talk to a man in a language he understands, that goes to his head. If you talk to him in his language, that goes to his heart.

Nelson Mandela

The ex-mayor, it soon became apparent, didn't trust anyone except his own family, so his sons and sons-in-law were the only ones to guard Des whilst under his care. They were all married; one had two wives and four or five children. They were farmers who lived in the mountains, so they had no experience of dealing with foreigners. Their vision of life was limited to their own world. Des spent as much time as possible talking to them, trying to build up a relationship.

One of the guards, who was about thirteen, had never gone to school. He didn't know how to read or write, but he knew everything about guns. He carried an Armalite and had undergone military training. That was his entire world. He was a son of the commander known as 'Batman'. Des watched him play pretend-shooting in the open, saying 'boop boop boop' as he swung the gun around, but unlike most young boys that Des knew, this boy had a real gun in his hand. He wasn't pulling the trigger, but he was going through the fantasy that many young people go through at that particular stage of life.

As can sometimes happen with hostages, Des started to feel sympathetic towards his abductors. He hated being a prisoner, but he understood that they believed they would not have been listened to by the government had they not taken him captive. He wondered if they were right.

His diary entry that day read:

Thursday, 30th October

From the early morning BBC World Service I learn that Ireland drew with Belgium. My new home is a hut about six by eight feet with galvanized roof and sides of leaves. Breakfast: dried fish and rice. We went to the river to wash. I had only a tiny piece of soap left so I could not wash my clothes properly. Shortly after noon the rain began and continued until nightfall. I spent the time trying to keep the rain off my bed. My guards, except one boy of about 13, are men in their early twenties. Conversation is about their poverty of life in the mountains and religion. Sex is also a major topic, particularly their fantasies of marrying beautiful white women. I am coming to realise the importance of being positive, being strengthened by God's love rather than feeding on the rising resentment inside myself about being kept captive.

The next two days passed peacefully for the guards and Des began to relax somewhat. They went to the river first thing in the morning to wash, and then sat in the sun for a while, which was a great relief from the dark and dankness of the thick forest. When they returned to the hut to get breakfast on the first morning, the local sultan was at the hut with a letter from Aleem Elias Macarandas. Elias had come to see Des, but the kidnappers wouldn't allow him in, so he sent a letter to him, assuring him he was in safe hands. He also sent some supplies: biscuits and several bottles of mineral water. There was some assurance in that. This was the fruit of a relationship that had been built up over several years. Des took comfort from the fact that there were concerned people trying to help him and working on the negotiations.

The local sultan also brought him a large notebook, which

Des was delighted with, as the pieces of yellow paper he had been writing his diary on were almost gone. That afternoon in the hut, Des discovered that some of the guards were interested in learning some English phrases, so he agreed to teach them. They started with Maranao, then Visayan, which he then translated into English.

The guards tried to learn the words and pronounce them properly. One fellow in particular was quite interested, and they spent the whole afternoon working on that. It was a welcome distraction for the prisoner, even though the English they really wanted to learn was mostly about how they would propose to a white woman. The conversation often got back to sex. Des found that they couldn't go through a half-hour conversation without it coming up some way or another.

As he spent more time with them, he learned they were simple farmers who were uninvolved in the abduction, other than being used to guard him because they knew the terrain and were related to the ex-mayor. One of them, Mala (the ex-mayor's son-in-law), was very friendly and confided that his wife had given birth to two children, but both died within days of being born. The babies had some rare disease. Des told him the Mercy Sisters ran a good hospital in Iligan and that he should bring her there if she got pregnant again, as they may be able to help.

Des also enjoyed keeping them on their toes sometimes. On one occasion they talked about the possibility of them meeting another group and how they might give him a gun.

'No,' Des said, 'don't give me a gun.'

'Why not?'

'I might shoot one of you,' he replied, keeping his face deadly serious.

Later that day, when they were down at the river, a guard called Elias started putting on a display of his strength. He lifted

8 November 1991. The installation of Fr Des Hartford in the cathedral in Marawi as apostolic administrator of Marawi.
© *Neil Collins/Columban Missionaries*

September 1969 in Bayside, New York. Frs Rufus Halley, John Brazil and Donie Hogan on their way to the Philippines for the first time.
© *Donie Hogan/Columban Missionaries*

A view of houses near the shore of Lake Lanao in the
Islamic city of Marawi.
© Jean Harrington

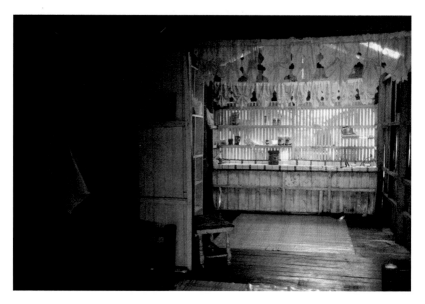

Inside a house in Marawi. The simplicity of how many people lived in the
Philippines was a contrast to Irish society. Rufus, in particular, always strove
to live close to the poverty that the local people experienced.
© Jean Harrington

Fr Rufus Halley teaching and laughing with community leaders in Our Lady of Peace High School, Malabang, 1996. Rufus was always very popular with the students in the school. © *Donie Hogan/Columban Missionaries*

May 1999. Venus (*left*), Rufus and other Filipina lay missionaries, Sancha and Eden, on a visit to Ireland. Venus became friends with Rufus while she was a student in Marawi State University, and they remained close friends for the rest of his life. © *Columban Missionaries*

Cagayan de Oro, 2005. Sr Celia Eco, who was one of Rufus's closest friends. They maintained their close friendship when they were apart through frequent letters. © *Jean Harrington*

Marawi, 2005. Author Jean Harrington with (*left to right*) Fr Yrap Nazareno, Sultan Lawan Minalang, Fr Paul Glynn and Sultan Maguid Maruhom.
© *Jean Harrington*

Marawi, 2005. *Left to right*: Moctar Matuan, Connie Balindong, Noriah Elias and friend. The friendships Rufus and Des made within the Muslim community were long-lasting. It was the richness of those friendships that helped keep Des safe during his kidnapping. © *Jean Harrington*

Accompanied by Archbishop Capalla, Fr Des Hartford addresses the media after being released from his captivity.
© *Donie Hogan/Columban Missionaries*

7 November 1997. Des celebrates his freedom with friends, including Rufus Halley (*far left*), Donie Hogan (*left of Des*), Fr Michel de Gigord (*right of Des*) and Paul Glynn (*far right*).
© *Donie Hogan/Columban Missionaries*

Des relaxing with friends after his release.
© *Donie Hogan/Columban Missionaries*

Rufus Halley's funeral mass in Cagayan de Oro.
As he was carried out of the church they played one of his favourite songs,
'Time to Say Goodbye', sung by Andrea Bocelli and Sarah Brightman.
© Donie Hogan/Columban Missionaries

Rufus's five brothers flew to the Philippines for his funeral.
© Columban Missionaries

A motorbike was Rufus's favourite form of transport. He never wore a helmet when he rode between the parishes in Mindanao, but would protect his head from the sun with a soft, white hat. On this occasion, he was visiting the family of one of the Muslim students at Our Lady of Peace High School with Donie Hogan. © *Donie Hogan/Columban Missionaries*

Rufus Halley and Des Hartford's last meeting, in Carlow in June 2001, a few weeks before Rufus returned to the Philippines for the last time.
© *Columban Missionaries*

huge stones out of the river and put them on the riverbank so Des could sit on them in the sun.

'Thanks very much,' Des said.

That evening Elias started to complain about a pain in his groin.

'That's serious,' Des said. 'That's a hernia.'

'What do you mean?'

'If that becomes strangulated, the infection will drip down into your testicles and they might explode,' Des told him with a deadpan face. The guard wasn't sure if he was joking with him, but after a day or two he came to Des with a big smile saying his hernia was gone and he was okay.

***

On the third day in the hut, Des was listening to the sports report from London on BBC World Service on his small short-wave radio, when very heavy shooting resounded from the direction of the village. The guards became very fearful and said, 'Our instructions are that if there is any shooting we have to evacuate.' They had heard rumours that another armed group was planning on kidnapping Des for their own purposes. There were so many breakaway terrorist groups and individual bandits in Mindanao that this had been one of Des's biggest fears from the beginning. As a hostage to a group with a list of demands for the government, he felt his situation would not last long. If he was taken by another group, however, he had no idea how bad or how long his incarceration might be.

They packed everything quickly and moved down to the river, walking in the water as far as a marshy area. Mala went ahead, trying to make a path, but there was no trail and the branches kept flicking back into their faces. The guards were terrified, and this affected Des. His diary entry on Saturday 1 November attests to this: 'Today I experienced real fear.' But the guards didn't want anything to happen to him.

Mala said, 'Father, we'll die defending you. If it comes to it, we'll all die together.'

After about forty minutes of walking through the marshy area, something inside Des changed and he came to accept he might die that day. Once he accepted this, he was no longer afraid. It was very clear to Des that the guards weren't going to hand him over if someone did manage to catch up with them.

After about an hour and a half the shooting stopped. Mala took off his bullets, put down his guns and, putting on his cap, he went back into the village dressed as a farmer. He soon returned with a smile on his face. It had been a false alarm. One of the guns in the village, the 30-calibre machine gun, had gotten stuck, so they decided to test it but had forgotten to tell the men who were guarding Des.

Des had two reactions, one immediately after the other. The first was relief; the other was anger. *Why on earth didn't they tell us they were going to do the shooting?* he thought.

The guards wanted to return to the hut, but Des spoke out at this stage. 'I'm not going back through the swamp, into the river and to the hut ... I am too tired!'

They were in an open space where they could see the mountain, and they weren't too far from the village as they had gone in a semi-circle around it. One of them replied, 'Okay, we'll wait here until it gets dark.'

About 6.30 p.m., after the sun had set, they brought Des to the ex-mayor's house, on the outskirts of the village. As they approached the house, they saw someone with a flashlight, who said a child in the house was sick and the herbal doctor was there. They didn't want the doctor to know about Des, so they hoisted the priest into an upstairs room at the back of the house.

Once inside, Des could hear talk from the front room. They were all talking about this priest who had been kidnapped and what a good guy he was, and what a pity it was he had been taken.

Once the doctor left, the family came in to have a look at Des, including the ex-mayor, who still wore his balaclava for some reason, even though his wife and children didn't hide their faces. Des's diary entry for that day reflected how he was constantly thinking about escaping:

> All the members of the family came to have a look at me. Security is light. Escape would be possible, except for the fact that everyone in the surroundings is on the side of my guards.

He slept there that night, delighted to be in a house with a proper bed. It rained and rained so he was very grateful to be properly sheltered. He also stayed there most of the next day and was able to read, relax and reflect. During these times he found great power in reading the word of God.

A few days before he was taken, he had been on a retreat in Marawi where he reflected on the phrase in Psalm 138: 'With your strength O Lord, you have strengthened me.' These words came back to Des several times during his first few days of captivity; you cannot rely on only your own strength in these situations, you have to rely on God to strengthen you. It was this source of strength that allowed him to go on. He found that texts from the Bible came forcefully to his consciousness before they were needed, almost as if they were guided to him just before the relevant situation arose.

One of the guards came into Des's room in the afternoon.

'What's your favourite soup?'

'Oh gosh, we have a menu tonight! Things are looking up.'

'No,' he said. In Visayan dialect he had said *sabon*. 'What's your favourite soap?' *Sabao* is the word for soup, and they sounded very similar to Des.

He started to laugh, because he had been thinking excitedly of whether he'd ask for mushroom or vegetable soup. He spent most of that day in his bedroom and finished *Towards Zero*, the Agatha Christie novel.

The guards asked him to write a message, which they said they would fax to the Columbans. They thought it would speed up the negotiations if Des told them he was likely to be released as soon as the kidnappers' demands were met.

Des was happy to have the opportunity to send a message to his friends and family, and wrote the following, which they subsequently faxed to Archbishop Capalla. An extract of the message appeared in *The Irish Times*:

> Up to the present moment I am in good health and good spirits. I am being treated well by my guards considering the circumstances in which I am living. They are doing all they can to make my stay here comfortable. My worry is that I might get sick but I have experienced no fear from my captors. The only danger is from the military or some other group who might try to rescue me.
>
> To the best of my knowledge the rebel returnees have legitimate demands already approved. If this is so, I hope they can be met as soon as possible.
>
> Please assure my family and friends that I am keeping up my spirits. I am in good health and I hope to be released soon.[1]

The paper also reported Fr Noel Connolly, the vicar general of the Columbans, saying he 'was still optimistic that he will be released unhurt, but I don't know how long it will take'. In the same interview, Connolly said, 'The government don't want to give in to blackmail or kidnapping but want to do the right thing.' He pointed out that there were also genuine difficulties in the situation because grants were reportedly being claimed by those who were not rebels. The government also suggested that others had claimed for many people but had then refused to pass the payments on to the rightful owners.

Connolly concluded by emphasising the point that it was crucial the military did not get involved. 'We will use our influence to try to keep pressure on the Philippine government. We appreciate what they are doing and as long as this has international backing, the military will not intervene.'

The local papers in Manila also continued to report on the situation and the *People's Tonight* headline said: 'MILF encircles Irish bishop captors'. The article quoted Al Haj Murad, the MILF vice-chairman for military affairs, as saying, 'We have encircled them to prevent them from escaping and getting the priest out of the area.'[2]

At the time of Des's kidnapping, the MILF was trying to promote itself with the Organisation of Islamic Cooperation (OIC) as being worthier than the MNLF to represent the cause of Filipino Muslims.[3] Before they could try to be recognised by the OIC, however, they needed the approval of the Philippine government, which is why they wanted to do the 'good deed' of trying to help secure Des's release by surrounding the kidnappers.

The article went on to say that the Department of the Interior and Local Government's team negotiating Des's release had returned empty-handed from its mission. Secretary Robert Barbers had flown to Lanao the previous Wednesday after being directed by President Ramos to personally supervise the ongoing negotiations. The article listed the benefits due to the rebel returnees, as told by the chairman and president of the Philippine Rebel Returnees Association, Camar 'Arenel' Cabugatan.

This was not a simple matter of someone being kidnapped by bandits. Des hoped the government would resolve the situation decisively, so that the rebel returnees would not feel forced to take similar drastic action again in the future.

***

On the second night in the ex-mayor's house, there was a commotion with people coming and going. About 4 a.m. a guard barged into Des's room and said, 'Get ready; we have to go before it is light.'

They left quickly and went through the village. Des noticed some people going into the mosque. They went out again into the countryside, towards the plateau rather than the forest. They brought him into the brush and hid him there.

This was one of his hardest days, and was a particularly low point for Des as he had a lot of time to think in uncomfortable surroundings. He started to feel sorry for himself, and his diary entry for the day captured those thoughts:

Monday, 3rd November

It's a very difficult day. I feel so tired. I think I am almost at breaking point. It is as much mental and emotional fatigue as physical. In the early afternoon I cried. It is my first time to cry in 3 years, that is, since the death of Lydia Macas who was killed in our house by a grenade. I tried to conceal the fact that I was crying from the guards. After crying I felt a bit better. Everything is now turned over to the Lord. I can only go on in the strength and the power of the Lord. I have not arrived at the stage where I can equally accept life or death. I still want to live and I'm afraid of the pain of a violent death.

He tried to hold on to all the positive experiences he had had with his Muslim friends in the past, and he thought back to when he lived with Lawan in the *barrio* and how he had been accepted as a fellow human being, without there being a 'Christian' label on him.

At around 4 p.m. one of the guards, Elias, came back and said, 'There's a change of plan. You're going to be taken into the camp of the Moro Islamic Liberation Front.'

The MILF had a camp in the area and Des was to be handed over to them – for safekeeping, so he was told. By this stage, Des was too exhausted to care about who was guarding him; he only cared that he was still a prisoner. He had no idea that officials in the MILF were cooperating with the government on one hand, while also working with the MNLF on the other in order to help protect their hostage. He only knew that terrorist groups worked together sometimes when it suited their purposes. Despite what the MILF was telling the government and the public, this was indeed one of those times.

They walked through the village very openly, and people seemed to appear from everywhere. They stayed for about thirty minutes at the ex-mayor's house. All the children gathered around with great curiosity. He was tired and didn't want to talk to people, yet everyone was there to look at him. All the women and the children were making a great racket. He complained to the guards that he had had enough of this type of thing. He wasn't in the right shape to deal with them, although the kids weren't doing anything out of the ordinary, other than looking at an 'Americano' with a long nose, making jokes and so on.

'Father, whether you like it or not, you cannot stop the music,' was the pragmatic reply he received.

They then took him to the MILF camp, which turned out to be only about thirty minutes from the village. They believed Des would be safer there, as the army would not expect him to be in a MILF stronghold. There were around forty heavily armed men in the camp with outposts, machine guns and two-way radio contact. The camp was just a two-storey building, with the lower storey open to the elements. It had one big floor area, where a number of women and children played together.

Des was turned over to the commander, Jaheeja, and they gave him a little place in the corner where he could lie down and rest. He talked for hours, as everyone wanted to hear his story. Once the sun went down, the call to prayer took place, and a number of the armed guards put their guns down and prayed.

Des went to bed early and slept, despite the commotion caused by everyone talking around him. At about 12.30 a.m. he needed to go to the toilet, so he stepped over sleeping bodies to get out. On his return, he noticed there were still two or three people talking in the room, one of whom was an old, very talkative woman. Des was completely awake at this stage, so he listened to her as he returned to his corner. She was chewing a betel nut, and her gums had gone red and drawn. She looked rusty in her appearance, in every sense of the word.

She began chanting an epic poem of the Maranaos, the *Darangan*, which has been transcribed into eight volumes. Every fifteen minutes she'd take a break and give a big spit into a spittoon she had beside her.

Des was pretending to be asleep, but he was listening. There was a guard on watch, who analysed every part with her for about five minutes before she'd start again, on the next part. This went on and on and on. She was deeply immersed in her religious faith and her oral culture. Des was beginning to wonder if she was going to chant all eight volumes.

It reminded him of an advertisement that had run in Ireland for paint with the punchline 'Rust never sleeps'. *This Rusty never sleeps*, Des thought to himself with a wry smile. He dropped off eventually and slept until he was wakened by the call to prayer at 4.30 a.m.

CHAPTER 13

Faith makes things possible, not easy.

Luke 1:37

The people working to secure Des's release spanned both sides of the globe and there was a concerted effort between them all to ensure the military did not try to reach Des. There was a very real danger that any attempted rescue by the military would result in a shoot-out between the army and the kidnappers, and Des would get caught in the crossfire. With this in mind, on 28 October 1997, several people contacted President Ramos.

Donie Hogan wrote a letter to Ramos, asking for his help to ensure the safe and speedy release of Des. This letter was hand delivered by Nene Guevara, the undersecretary for finance, who was a friend of the Columbans. The Irish Embassy in Beijing also sent a fax to the president on the same day, expressing concern that 'Monsignor Hartford may be in considerable danger'. Archbishop Oscar Cruz, the president of the Catholic Bishops' Conference of the Philippines, also made representations to Ramos to help facilitate Des's speedy release and to give the rebels the grants they had been promised.

President Ramos took the interventions seriously. After the Cabinet meeting, Nene Guevara went directly to the Columban Central House in Singalong Street in Manila. She reported that all the communications had arrived and the president was very concerned about Des's plight. He was taking urgent action to help secure Des's immediate and safe release.

The rebels had requested that Archbishop Capalla negotiate on their behalf with the government. Capalla was the head of

Muslim–Christian relations for the Catholic Bishops' Conference of the Philippines and had an excellent reputation among the rebels as a fair and honest person.

On 30 October, President Ramos issued a press statement, emphasising that 'the safe recovery of Monsignor Hartford is paramount and therefore negotiations will be the main effort'. The national paper, *The Philippine Daily Inquirer*, carried a statement from Defence Secretary Fortunato Abat in which he ruled out any military rescue operation saying, 'these might put Hartford's life in danger'. The message was clear and was carried by all media nationwide.

On 2 November, Donie Hogan faxed a letter to Joe Hayes, Irish Ambassador to the Philippines and China, asking for his help:

> If the rebel returnees (or the MILF who some say are now holding Des) do not accept the conditions and therefore refuse to release Des immediately as demanded, then I think some more clout is needed down here … At this stage I think we need the personal involvement of someone of your stature. I have heard that on Tuesday, November 4, there will be a meeting of EU Ambassadors in Manila. Is it possible for you to attend and make representations on behalf of Des?[1]

Hayes immediately responded positively, saying he would do all he could to help.

In the meantime, Des's friend Aleem Elias Macarandas had become involved in negotiations for Des's freedom. He heard that Des had been turned over to the MILF commander Jaheeja. Elias convinced the MILF and the kidnappers to surrender Des to the authorities. He then travelled to Cagayan de Oro to attend a four-hour meeting, trying to iron out the details of Des's release with Archbishop Capalla, solicitor Alberto Bernardo, Mahid Mutilan, senior politicians, and representatives of the rebels.

Things appeared to be happening quickly, as Donie received a phone call from General Nazareno the next day, informing him that Des was to be released the following day – Tuesday 4 November. Donie had been liaising with Des's family in Ireland, keeping them up to date with the news. When he heard that Des was about to be released, he was so relieved and thankful to have some good news he decided to tell Des's family straight away. Up to this point he had been the bearer of bad news, so he took it upon himself to ring Mary Comiskey, Des's sister, in Rush in Co. Dublin.

'Mary, it's Donie. I finally have some good news,' he said in his soft Waterford accent. 'They are about to release Des. I'm heading to Mindanao now to see if I can be there when he's released.'

'That's great news, Father,' Mary replied. 'Thank you!'

'I'll keep you informed of what happens,' Donie promised as he hung up.

He immediately flew to Cagayan de Oro, in northern Mindanao, where he met Archbishop Capalla. He told him about the possible involvement of the EU ambassadors in trying to facilitate Des's release, but Capalla became alarmed, as he feared this sort of high-level international intervention could encourage more abductions in the future. The EU had many major projects in the area that could be targeted. And there was the prospect of more priests being snatched, too.

Donie started to panic as he contemplated the reality of Capalla's words. He had no access to a fax machine, so he hurriedly phoned the Columban Central House in Manila, asking that a fax be sent immediately to Joe Hayes in Beijing to say that matters had changed dramatically and he was now advising him not to come to Manila.

Peter Steen, a former Columban regional director, got Donie's message. Realising the urgency, he immediately sent a fax to the Irish ambassador, the gist of which was, 'Donie Hogan says don't come!'.

Joe was about to leave for the airport when the fax arrived. He trusted Donie's judgement, so he simply unpacked and remained in Beijing, awaiting further developments.

***

Early the next morning, 4 November, Capalla and Donie headed to Kolambugan parish, a four-hour journey from Cagayan de Oro. This was where Des was expected to be brought upon his release. Kolambugan is in the province of Lanao del Norte and has a population of about 29,000 people. Major General Joselin Nazareno and regional police chief Dominador Resos were already gathered with other officials. They spent a long, frustrating day in the parish house waiting for Des, but from their point of view, nothing happened.

Des, on the other hand, was kept busy, unaware of the negotiations that were taking place on his behalf while he overnighted in the MILF camp with the Rusty who didn't sleep. On the morning of 4 November, while Donie and his friends waited for him to be released, he was allowed to wash with a hose – his first wash in three days. He also received a package from his friends in Marawi that contained rosary beads, his Bible and a breviary.

When he was with the guards he overheard a conversation on the two-way radio. Someone said he was a priest, a missionary, and that he had nothing to do with the government. The person on the radio said he was to be protected and asked why they were not releasing him. The guards didn't reply to the radio but told Des to pack. They said the army was approaching, so they moved him back to the village, where he was returned to the MNLF, under the ex-mayor's care.

Later that day, two MILF men arrived from Lanao del Sur with copies of *The Philippine Daily Inquirer*, which said that Des would be released soon. It was four days old and he still hadn't been released; he was now on his ninth day of captivity.

His guards, Mala and Juan, soon realised that the men from Lanao del Sur were up to no good; indeed, they were the advance party for a much bigger group that wanted to take Des and bring him back to Lanao del Sur to use him for their own ends. Des's greatest fear now seemed like a very real possibility. Acting fast, Mala and Juan immediately got him out of the house and, from that particular point on, they were on the run from these renegade Lanao del Sur rebels.

He walked with his guards for about forty-five minutes until they reached a house on its own, not in the forest but on rolling land. To Des's great surprise, in the sea of Muslims, they took him to the only Christian family in the area. Des couldn't understand why they would go to Christians with an abducted priest.

'Why did you bring me here?' he asked.

They told him that the people who were looking for him would not have believed Des's guards would trust Christians, so it seemed an obvious choice to them. Hiding in plain sight. Despite believing they would probably be safe in the house, they still went through a thorough preparation in case anyone checked it. Des was to act as the grandfather who was not to be disturbed, as he was sick and under a blanket with the flu. If someone knocked at the door, the young man and his wife would go and see who it was while the guards stayed inside.

The couple had a little girl, who was about three years of age and very chatty. Her parents were trying to warn her, so they started doing a role-play with her to see how she would react if someone came looking for Des.

'If anybody comes, what are you going to say?'

'I will say, Lolo Padre is not here,' she said, clearly delighted with the attention.

Lolo Padre translated into grandfather priest, so Des started laughing but said, 'Don't say that. Just say Lolo José is here.'

It was a great relief for him to speak in the Christian dialect of Visayan again, as he was more comfortable in this language. For the first time in days, he relaxed a little bit.

The guards asked Des to write another note, this time to Governor Dimaporo. Des obliged and wrote a letter, requesting him to forego political aims. He also asked that the army not get directly involved in his release. He gave the letter to Mala, then went looking for the man of the house.

Des had about thirty pesos in his pocket. During his entire captivity, no one had actually searched him or taken anything from him. He slipped the man of the house ten pesos and asked him to kill a chicken for him. He said he was starving. He asked the man's wife if she could cook some vegetables. She replied she would make him some corn on the cob.

Because Des didn't trust that he would ever be released, his mind was constantly on how to get out of captivity. He saw that the farmer had a horse, and realised it might be an opportunity to escape. He talked to the man about it.

'How far is it to the nearest Christian villages? And would it be possible for me to get there?'

The Christian man wasn't interested in helping Des escape. He was afraid and said it would still be very difficult. Des knew he couldn't escape without this man's knowledge of the local area.

Suddenly there was an alert. The guards had spotted a group

and said they had to go. Des put his foot down. 'I'm going to eat. I'm waiting for my dinner.'

The vegetables and soup were ready, so the guards relented slightly and said he could eat those before they left. Des quickly ate corn on the cob, along with the soup, then they left the house and hid in a nearby ravine.

He captured his feelings in that day's diary entry:

Tuesday, 4 November 1997

I prayed as best I could. Around 6am I got my first wash in three days from a hose downstairs. Continual conversation on the two-way radio. My release always seems to be 'tomorrow'. My Bible, breviary and rosary beads that I had requested were brought from Marawi. At 8am I was told to pack. The army were approaching. I was taken back to the house near the village. Feeling very low. A group of people on their way back to a mountain village came to look at me. One of them encouraged me to escape.

Their leader sat on the bed and every now and then he would spit through a tiny vent in the wall. If ever there was an international spitting contest the Maranaos would get the gold medals for accuracy. At 4.30pm I was told to pack again. All this moving is exhausting. A 30 minute walk to a small house where a little girl talked non-stop to me.

Some rebel returnees are not satisfied with the agreement being worked out. They have brought 100 armed men to try to take me. I am on the run with my guards. It is tiring and distressful because it has brought a new threat to my life.

'The snare has been broken and we have escaped.' That verse of the psalm gives me hope.

Although he wrote about having hope, the truth was it was a challenge for him to believe the text. He was exhausted and stressed. He wanted to believe that God's word would be fulfilled, that he would escape and be set free, but he couldn't see any end in sight.

***

Back in Kolambugan Donie spent the day in frustration, not knowing why Des had not been released. As each hour passed, he grew more disappointed, knowing in his heart that something had gone wrong. Finally, at about 10 p.m., word came through that there had been a hitch in negotiations and Des would not be released.

The next morning, a deeply disappointed Capalla headed back to Davao, while Donie returned dejectedly to Manila. Donie was so disappointed and embarrassed that he hadn't the heart to call Des's family, so he asked Noel Connolly, the vicar general of the Columbans in Dublin, to break the bad news to them instead.

Later, police intelligence sources said the hitch in the negotiations arose on 3 November because several politicians in the region wanted Des released to them to promote their individual political aims, and the kidnappers were divided on who to turn the priest over to. Tensions were high and, because the impasse was getting worse, Elias advised the kidnappers not to release Des to a political party.

Because the MILF decided not to release Des to the politicians, the military suddenly advanced on the camp on the morning of 5 November. Elias suspected it was at the behest of certain politicians but, by the time the army reached the camp, Des was, of course, already gone.

Des's friends were concerned there would be a shoot-out if the army caught up with the MILF members who had been holding Des, so Elias's friend Nasali Nung, who was involved in the negotiations, asked the army to pull back about one kilometre from the camp, so they could safely access it.

Elias and his fellow negotiators then asked the MILF to turn Des over to the authorities. However, there was conflict and disagreement between the overall MILF command, which was happy for Des to be released, and the local MILF group controlling Des's freedom, who didn't agree with releasing him. They refused to tell the others where they were keeping Des and that they had already handed him back to MNLF guards.

Meanwhile, in Ireland the government was working to ensure he would be set free swiftly and without harm. On 5 November Minister for Foreign Affairs David Andrews met the Philippine Ambassador to Britain with responsibility for Ireland to convey the government's anxiety about Des's safety. Members of Des's family attended, along with Columban Superior General Nicholas Murray and Vicar General Noel Connolly. Andrews urged the government of the Philippines to maintain their efforts to resolve the situation in a peaceful manner.

***

While the meeting was taking place in Dublin, it was getting dark in the mountains in Mindanao and Des was told he had to start moving again. This was one of the most difficult nights for him because he was forced to walk for about four or five hours. They walked along the trail, moving away from the village, along the plateau and towards a Christian area. They often passed houses, disturbing dogs who barked. This frightened the guards, so they would go off the trail, detour and then get back on the trail again. At one stage they were walking in the forest when they said, 'Drop down!'

'What is it?' Des asked.

'There's a horse coming.'

Des didn't hear anything, but he obeyed nevertheless, as he had come to trust their sensitive hearing. He dropped and eventually the horse came along and galloped off into the night. Luckily it was merely a farmer sitting atop it. After another two hours they went off the trail into a ravine. They paused here to rest and eat under the shelter of banana trees. The guards had some rice and Des ate as many bananas as he could. He was constantly hungry during his captivity.

About midnight they arrived at a cornfield. 'We have to sleep here,' one of the guards said. 'You have to take off your shoes going in to make sure there are no marks.'

Des couldn't see the sense in it. 'If I take off my shoes I'll make more marks because of the muck.'

The guards were not going to humour him, and Des could sense this, so without further discussion he took off his boots, put on his flip-flops and went into the cornfield, slipping and sliding all the way.

They went deep into the field, where the rows of corn were around six feet high. They cut the stalks off some in the middle of the field and put down the tarpaulin as a bed for Des, with his mosquito net over it. Des found it very difficult and uncomfortable, however, as he was very constricted in his movement.

While he was trying to get comfortable, one of the guards, Abdul, came quietly to him and asked how much Des would pay him if he let him go free. He said that when it was his turn to guard at night, he could guide him to a car and drive to Cagayan de Oro.

Although Des desperately wanted to escape, and had often thought seriously about it, he was ultimately very conscious that he wanted to be able to return to Marawi when this was all over. He knew if something like that happened he would never be able to return; he'd be a target because he had outwitted them. He didn't want it to end that way, he realised, particularly when there was no pressure on him or the Columbans to provide the money. The pressure was all on the government.

Des tried to discourage the guard without insulting him. 'You don't seem to have thought out the consequences of this, either for yourself or for me. First of all, for yourself. You're a married man. They're all going to be angry with you because they didn't get the money. And you're going to walk away with only a certain, small amount of money. You won't be able to come back here.'

Abdul began to think about it. Des was also mindful of the fact that the guard may have been just setting him up. He wasn't sure if Abdul was trying to find out if he had plans to escape.

'It's not a great idea because we have a long, long way to go before we'd even make it out to the road where you could get transport. It's a whole day or a whole night's journey and we're within territory where I would be recognised immediately as a foreigner and probably as the person who had been kidnapped.'

Abdul agreed, and left him alone after that.

That evening the guards came to Des. 'We have to move, we've been in the same place all day and they could have tracked us.'

The guards were very concerned about being followed or tracked. They sent Mala ahead as an advance guard when they travelled through the forest. He was very sensitive to movement and could hear people coming and see things Des wouldn't be able to see immediately. That day he went ahead on the trail, as usual, but after a short time he came running back and said, 'There's a group coming.'

Elias grabbed Des's arm and they ran off the trail, down the side of a ravine, slipping and sliding. Whenever Des fell, Elias pulled him up. Eventually they lay flat in the ravine.

After about twenty minutes Mala went up and checked what was happening. When he returned he said, 'It's okay! They are gone. They have passed us by.'

'How many were in the group?'

'About thirty armed men.'

Later on, he found out the group had gone directly to where he had been all day and that psalm he'd been thinking about came alive for him. 'The snare has been broken and we have escaped.'

At this point, he couldn't take much more. His mind became hyperactive and he felt that he was hurtling towards a mental precipice.

He knew he would not survive much longer.

CHAPTER 14

When it gets dark enough, you can see the stars.

Charles A. Beard

Eventually Des fell asleep and slept for about three hours. He was shaking when he awoke and thought he had flu or a high fever, but he was just trembling with the cold. *This is the bloody end*, he thought. He saw that the heads of the corn were leaning over the top of the mosquito net and the dew was dripping down on him, which had caused him to get a chill. He put on his T-shirt and jacket and eventually, when the dawn came, the guards made coffee on a little gas stove. He felt better with the heat of the sun on his face and thought he could cope with whatever the day brought. It was now Thursday 6 November, his eleventh day in captivity.

With the dawn they realised that, although they were hidden by the corn, there was a coconut grove just beside the field on a hill, and anyone who was in the coconut grove could see right in.

'We have to move, we have to get out of here.'

They made him wear a black jacket with a balaclava once they left the cornfield as a precaution. The guards were very tense and listening to every sound. On the route, they met a man and, as had happened with other passers-by, they told him in no uncertain terms that his throat would be slit if he told anyone about them.

They didn't like moving around in daylight, but they had no choice. They walked through a tributary river for about an hour to hide their trail and continued up the other side into the forest, where they stayed for the rest of the day. Des was exhausted.

When they stopped, Des was told if they went any further,

they could be discovered, so they had to stay where they were, although the area was very limited in size.

At one stage, Des heard some sounds, but everybody else was quite relaxed.

'What is it?' he asked.

'Oh, that's only monkeys.'

After about two minutes a group of monkeys came jumping through the trees. Des was amazed how his guards knew the sounds and were able to detect where the danger was with such ease and confidence.

That day in the forest, he took out his Bible and prayed for the Lord to give him a text that would sustain him. He opened the book at the last ten verses of the story of Lazarus (John 11:34–44). He started reading and two phrases jumped out at him: 'Loose his bonds and let him go free' and 'Lazarus come forth'. He hoped the text was right.

That night, he was so weak he told his captors, 'I have to sleep in a house tonight. I won't survive another night in the open. I have to sleep in a house.'

'It's impossible,' Juan said. 'At least 300 people are searching for you. If you sleep in a house, they are sure to find you because they are searching all the houses.'

'What we've decided to do is to build you a little tent in the bush, in the cogon grass, that you can sleep in on your own and we'd be at strategic points around you, but you'll be on your own,' one of the guards told him.

Mala crawled in under the nearby bush, where the undergrowth was quite heavy, and Des crawled in after him. He showed Des the little tent.

'I'll fix it so that nobody will know there's a trail, and they'll never find you as long as you stay quiet. You're not to make any sound. If anyone calls or comes near, you're not to say anything.'

The tent was only about two feet high. He couldn't even sit up in it; all he could do was lie down. It was on a slope, so either his head or feet were elevated. He had his bag with him and he decided to take off his jacket and change his T-shirt, as it was wringing wet with sweat. As he struggled with his belongings it struck him. *This is like a grave. This is the Lazarus thing: it's as if I'm buried in this place.* The text suddenly came back to him.

I'm going to get out of this alive, he thought.

It took him about half an hour to change because he was so weak and tired. He was also hungry, and he knew there was bread in his bag, so he went to take it out. The plastic around it crackled loudly every time he touched it. It reverberated through the silent forest. He hesitated for a moment and debated whether to open it or not, but eventually he got the plastic and ripped it open. 'To hell with the noise,' he muttered.

Some moments later, he heard a sound in the undergrowth, from the opposite direction to where Mala had gone, and he thought it may have been a monkey or something. It came closer and closer to where he was and suddenly stopped about ten metres from his tent. Des stayed completely still and silent. Eventually, after about ten minutes, he heard snoring. *Well, now, that must be Mala,* Des thought. *He must have crawled over there and gone asleep.*

His guards could sleep in absolutely any condition, even with mosquitoes savagely eating them. It really brought home to Des what the Americans were up against in Vietnam. These locals could live for days on nothing but rice and water. They could survive easily in the mountains in these totally primitive conditions – without any shelter.

As dawn was breaking the following morning, Des concentrated on praying. He felt he wouldn't survive, either mentally or physically, for much longer. He resented the inhuman confinement, and he found himself focusing once more on the words of St Paul (2 Corinthians 12:10): 'When I am weak, then I am strong.'

He had slept a little bit, despite the difficult conditions. In the morning Mala came along with a glass of boiling water.

'There's coffee in your bag, Father. Make yourself a coffee.'

Des was delighted.

Then Mala said, 'Peace time.'

'What do you mean?'

'They're all gone, all the people that were looking for you.'

He later learned that although several groups under the MILF umbrella were trying to capture him and use him for their own purposes, when they realised the top commanders within the MNLF had negotiated the terms of Des's release, they backed off. It wasn't worth their while to get into a war with the MNLF.

'The official MILF group who were tracking us now realise that the thing is almost over, and they don't want to endanger your life. So the groups that were looking for you are gone. It's almost over.'

Des felt a great relief and said, 'Can I come out?'

'No, just wait a while yet. We're still monitoring.'

After about an hour, two guards came over. Des couldn't see anything, as he was still in his makeshift tent. Then they said, 'You can come out now.'

As Des began to crawl out of his coffin-like tent, he thought about Lazarus. It didn't feel like the triumphant resurrection he had imagined. He was too down and tired. He just sat for a few minutes at the side of the tent, trying to gather some energy.

The guards began to clean it all up. They told him he could crawl out through the undergrowth and wait for them at the trail. He began to feel better once he was able to stand up and see the sun and mountains. Soon they were walking again.

They came to a coconut grove, and the guards gave him a coconut, which he mixed with sugar from his bag. As he ate the coconut and looked at the sunlight, he finally began to feel uplifted.

'Where are we going?' he asked.

'We're going back to the house. The negotiations are almost over, it's almost complete and you can just rest there.'

They brought him back to the Christian family's house, and Des said he wanted to wash. He was covered in dirt and sweat from his time in the forest; he desperately wanted to clean himself.

'Take it easy, Father, just relax. Lie on the bed for a while and we'll prepare a meal for you.'

He did as they asked and lay down while they prepared a nice meal of rice and carabao meat.

After he ate, Mala brought up the topic of washing. 'We don't want you to wash outside,' he said, 'because there will be too many people gathering to watch, so we need you to wash in the corner of the room.'

They brought in several gallons of water, and Des washed himself slowly, the water trickling through the floorboard slats. Afterwards, he felt quite refreshed. He even shaved and had a siesta. When he woke up he switched on his short-wave radio about 2.30 p.m. and listened to a programme about Mendelssohn on BBC World Service.

Suddenly a man ran into the room, grabbed him by the arm and said, 'We have to go, we have to go.'

Des was wearing nothing but a malong. He said, 'I want to put on my trousers.'

'No,' he said. 'We haven't time.'

Des felt like crying. 'I thought it was finished.'

The guard ignored Des's protestations and threw a woman's veil on him. They ran down the trail, with Des holding his malong with one hand and the woman's veil with the other. It briefly crossed his mind that he must have looked comical. They went back into the forest.

'What the hell is happening?' he asked once they'd stopped. 'I thought it was over!'

'There's an alarm. The army have come in and they're probably going to try to take you.'

'Flip it!'

'You stay here in the forest and we'll monitor it.'

They left him with two armed guards. After some time, Mala came with a very well-prepared chicken in some lovely chicken and vegetable soup. He said the Christian family had sent it. Des was delighted; food had never tasted so good to him.

Eventually a guard came to tell them it was a false alarm and they could return to the house. Some women from a neighbouring town had seen the army and thought it was coming into the village, but it had instead stopped at the boundary that had been agreed between it and the rebels. Des was relieved to hear the army was respecting the boundaries.

***

While this was going on, negotiations were taking place in the village. Elias and his fellow negotiators had come to the end of their successful negotiations with the MILF, who had agreed to hand Des over to the army. Before they would let him go, however, they demanded 200 pesos for what they had spent; they called it an accommodation fee. At the same time, senior commanders from the MNLF were negotiating with the government in Tangcal.

Once this was all agreed, Elias went to the army's chief of staff, General Nazareno, and the politicians. He told them, 'You must agree among yourselves how Des is to be released. After all, me and the people who were directly involved in the release of Des have no interest in that. We are not profiting or promoting our personalities. We do not want anything except the peaceful and safe release of Des.'

About 2 or 3 a.m. the group agreed that the military would receive Des from the kidnappers and then turn him over to the political leaders. There was no talk of a ransom being paid.

Elias didn't leave the place until he was sure Des would be released; once he was certain it was happening, he moved out of the area. On the way back to the house in Tangcal where he had spent the previous three nights, Elias replayed the situation in his head.

He was thankful the MILF had provided the security when needed and that the kidnappers didn't demand too much. He was grateful everyone had put Des's safety first and had worked together for his release. Despite his scepticism about certain politicians and the army, he knew they'd reconciled their initial differences in order to ensure the kidnap issue was safely ended.

When he reached Tangcal, he slept easily for the first time since he had heard the news of the kidnapping.

***

Mala told Des that the negotiations should be finished that afternoon, but he warned him if they didn't finish, they would likely break down completely, and Des would then be taken to Lanao del Sur.

Des responded to this news by asking Mala to pass on the information to the negotiators that he wouldn't survive much longer. He told them he had a heart condition and he couldn't go much further. It wasn't exactly untrue. The doctors had told him he had an enlarged heart, though he knew it wasn't anything serious.

'It has to finish today,' he said.

Eventually one of the guards said, 'Yes, it's finished; you can come up.'

As Des began putting things in his bag, the house became chaotic; there were all sorts of people milling around. The Christian family had arrived, so Des thanked them for the chicken and returned a copy of the Bible in Visayan that the guards had packed in his bag by mistake.

Eventually he was introduced to the person who had been the head negotiator in his release, a businessman from Zamboanga city called Alex Mavambi.

They shook hands.

'Thank you very much. I believe you were the one who finalised the negotiations.'

'That's okay, Father.'

'Is there anything I can do for you?' Des asked.

'No, thank you. Just look after yourself now, Father.' He leaned towards Des, his eyes narrowing. 'But Father, you must know that it's not totally over. Not yet. We're afraid of sniper fire, so it's important that you cover your head and stay silent as we lead you out of here, okay?'

Des nodded, suddenly anxious again. It was about 6.30 p.m. on Friday 7 November, and while he was no longer a prisoner, he still didn't feel safe.

Before he left, all the guards and people who had guarded him during his incarceration asked for forgiveness. Des didn't feel any deep feelings of anger against them. They had sworn they had nothing to do with the original plan; they were only asked to guard him because they were local to the area, they knew the terrain and they had some semblance of control over the people in the area.

Des was familiar with the concept of *gaba*, which exists in the

Philippines, particularly among the Muslim community. *Gaba* is a curse that brings bad luck to the person. There was a fear among the guards, particularly when they knew he was innocent, that Des would wish them evil. Juan was married to a Christian lady, and had a good command of Visayan, so he had the advantage of articulating that he wanted *pasaylo* (forgiveness). All wanted to part on good terms.

Des was surprised at his lack of bitterness.

'Yes. I forgive you because you've asked for it.'

He knew they were like him; they were only pawns.

Soon afterwards, Des and Alex walked into the forest with about four or five heavily armed guards walking ahead.

'Don't talk,' they warned as they walked along, Des's head covered once again with a malong. Alex walked behind him as he slowly made his way towards freedom.

Des felt a bit short-changed. It was supposedly all over, but he still had to walk! Eventually, after about two hours, they got to an agreed point, and the ex-mayor of Tangcal, who had been looking after him during eight of the eleven days, turned him over to the MILF. The MILF then handed him over to the army, who brought him down to the town of Tangcal. They went directly to the municipal hall, where the final negotiations were still taking place.

To his surprise there was a phone and fax machine in the hall. He was even more surprised to be given access to the phone.

It was about 12.30 a.m., but only about 4.30 p.m. in Ireland so he rang his brother, John, who lived in Lusk in Co. Dublin. His sister-in-law, Bernadette, answered the phone.

Des opened the conversation in his characteristic manner, brief and to the point.

'Bernie, I'm fine.'

He spoke briefly to his brother and asked him to ring the

superior general of the Columbans in Ireland, Fr Nicholas Murray, and to disseminate the news that he was free.

Governor Abdullah Dimaporo arrived at the hall in Tangcal about ten minutes later with a doctor and a nurse, who examined him to make sure he was well.

To his surprise, the MNLF commanders who had abducted him were also present, and were negotiating the final aspects of the agreement with the government and the army, although Commander Lakay Macabunta was conspicuous by his absence. Mamaki, the Black Panther and one of the other abductors were busy working things out with Dimaporo, while Des hovered restlessly in the background.

When everything appeared to be finalised, the third guard came to Des and asked him for forgiveness. Once again, Des gave the forgiveness that was asked, and then climbed into the ambulance that was waiting for him. It was about 4 a.m., and he quickly fell asleep in the ambulance, despite the bumpy road.

Finally, he was free.

**

Donie Hogan and Archbishop Capalla were on tenterhooks, waiting for news they could trust. Alberto Bernardo, who was working with the Columbans, contacted Capalla to say that his military sources believed Des would be released on 7 November, so Capalla and Donie flew back to Cagayan de Oro on the first morning flight. They spent the day once again in Kolambugan waiting for news, but heard nothing. Capalla stayed that night in Iligan with Bishop Bataclan, while Donie stayed with Paul Glynn in the Columban parish of Linamon.

Donie had just fallen asleep when he was woken by the phone shortly after 12.30 a.m. It was Noel Connolly calling from Ireland. He said, 'Des has been released.' Still half-asleep,

Donie replied, 'He hasn't been released. Paul Glynn and I have been here in Linamon all day awaiting news.'

Noel repeated, 'Donie, Des has been released. He telephoned his family a few minutes ago.'

Donie was afraid it was another false alarm but thanked Noel for the call. By this time Paul was awake, and as Donie shared the news with him, he began to hope it was true.

Ten minutes later, General Nazareno called confirming the good news that Des was released and would be brought by the military to Linamon in the early morning.

Before dawn the news had spread and Archbishop Capalla, Fr Rufil, Fr Michel Gigord, Rufus Halley, Sister Angie and some of the team from Marawi gathered with Paul and Donie on the balcony of the parish house in Linamon, waiting for Des.

At about 5 a.m. there was a rush of activity as military jeeps and pick-up trucks full of armed soldiers piled into the compound. The ambulance carrying Des came next. Capalla and Donie went down to greet him and accompany him upstairs to the balcony, where he was joyously and emotionally welcomed by his friends. It was just beginning to get light outside.

Once inside, Des was able to wash, have some food and relax with his friends for the next hour or two.

The governor was very anxious for Des to address the press, and had already arranged a press conference to take place in Cagayan de Oro, about a two-hour drive from Linamon. Des was driven to the Columban house there, where he read from a statement he had prepared while he was a prisoner, and addressed several of the issues that had bothered him during his incarceration:

> To those who betrayed my trust and my kindness and
> also to those rebel returnees who used me as a hostage, I

would like to remind you that what you did is against the true spirit of Islam. It was un-Islamic.

Your legitimate demands against the government should be made by legitimate means and not by the taking of innocent hostages.

To those in the government, both Christian and Muslim, and to those in other agencies who have failed to implement fully the agreements with rebel returnees, I would like to remind you that it is injustices like these that are a major reason for unrest between Muslims and Christians in Mindanao and Sulu.

Although my being taken hostage was a very painful experience, and contrary to freedom and other human rights, I still believe good will come from it. I encourage Muslims and Christians of goodwill of all levels to enter into a genuine dialogue with each other, so that together we can build a lasting peace here in Mindanao and Sulu that is based on justice, truth and love.[1]

III

UNDER A JACKFRUIT TREE

CHAPTER 15

The only thing we have to fear is fear itself.

Franklin D. Roosevelt

After lunch with his fellow Columbans and the team from Marawi who had gathered in Cagayan de Oro to welcome him, Des had a long siesta. He knew he would need some time to recover from his exhausting ordeal. He agreed with Donie Hogan that he needed time out in Ireland with his family to help him on his road to recovery, and he was conscious that they, too, had been through this ordeal with him and now needed to be with him.

Later that night, Rufus and Paul sat with Des and Donie. Rufus and Paul proposed to Des that he pay a short visit to Marawi before going to Ireland. They felt very strongly about this.

Des was uncomfortable with the idea. He was physically and mentally drained and felt he wasn't ready to place himself in a position of vulnerability. 'I'm not sure, Rufus,' he replied. 'I really don't know if I'm ready to get back into that situation.'

'But people really look up to you for your work in the dialogue,' Rufus gently said. 'You will have to go back at some point, and if you don't face it now, you might never be able to.'

'I think Rufus is right,' Paul said. 'If you allow the fear to take over, you might never return to Marawi, and you are needed there.'

'But the risk isn't only to Des,' Donie said. 'Everyone is exposed to this threat.'

They all nodded, allowing a moment for this point to sink in. Rufus went on to say that he was more committed than ever to the dialogue between Muslims and Christians and that he wouldn't let fear stop him from doing his job. Paul echoed these sentiments and declared that he would continue with his work in dialogue in Karomatan.

Donie, on the other hand, was so conscious of the risk of something happening to Des again that he strongly opposed Des returning to Marawi. He had been the one dealing with Des's family and the Columban superiors in Ireland, as well as the Irish ambassador in Beijing and the Irish media. He was very aware of the great support given by the Irish people to Des during his captivity, and he did not want to put them through such an experience again. He believed that if anything happened to Des in Marawi, the people at home would think the Columbans were fools to take such a risk and that he, as director, would be seen as being foolish for allowing Des to return to Marawi. In fact, he felt so strongly about it that he wanted to forbid Des from returning to Marawi, but he was not sure if he had the required authority, as Des's assignment as apostolic administrator was made by Rome and not by the Columbans.

Des listened intently to everyone's views and sat back quietly, contemplating their words. 'It's not that easy when you've had guns pressed against you for almost two weeks,' Des concluded. 'I'll think about going back to Marawi overnight and will let you know.'

The next morning he announced he would be going straight home to Ireland. Donie breathed a deep sigh of relief.

Later that morning, Donie met with Rufus and reiterated the point made the previous night. He said, 'Rufus, it's not only Des who is in danger. Anyone could be a target next. I feel you are very exposed in Malabang, for example.'

'Don't worry about me, Donie! Connie and her family have guaranteed my safety, and nobody will take on the Balindongs.'

Connie Balindong was one of several Muslims who had become a close friend of Rufus. She came from a powerful political family in Malabang. She worked in the school with him and was a friend to many of the Columbans. The two had first met when MSU opened the Southern Philippines Centre for Peace Studies, which hosted a seminar on Mindanao and Sulu cultures. Rufus enrolled on the course and moved into the bishop's house, where Connie was also staying. The two quickly became friends and, when she moved home to Malabang some time later, he visited her there every few weeks. Their friendship deepened when he moved to Malabang.

That evening Donie flew back to Manila to make arrangements for Des's departure for Ireland, and Des followed a few days later. From there he soon flew home.

While in Ireland, Des spent some much-needed time with his family, recuperating physically and mentally. He was contacted by the national television broadcaster, RTÉ, which made a documentary on his kidnapping and broadcast it as part of the *Would You Believe?* series. On the programme Des spoke about his difficulties in coming to terms with what had happened, and he recounted how he had refused to shake hands with Lakay's wife.

One day while he was out walking in Lusk, he was approached by an old lady who lived in the village.

'Father,' she said, grabbing him by the arm. 'Fr Dessie! Me knees was worn out prayin' for yah! And I'm glad you didn't give that woman forgiveness.'

Des couldn't help himself; he laughed.

'Thank you. I was very conscious of the prayer and the power of the prayers of the people, and that has been verified very much since I came home. The fact that many, many people have told me that they did pray for me. I was conscious and strengthened by the prayer of the people.'

He also recorded an interview with Fr Dan O'Malley to document his experience. He addressed his fears of returning to Marawi.

'To face going back, I think the overall thing is that it has been a deep faith experience. The Lord has looked after me in that particular situation. I should have and I do have more trust and more hope that I can continue what the Lord is asking me to do, and yet I do have apprehensions about going back. I would be hopeful I can continue the work of dialogue between Muslims and Christians.'[1]

He spent Christmas with his brother in Lusk, but knew he couldn't stay away from the Philippines for much longer. As the apostolic administrator in Marawi, he was a person of authority and a lot of people were waiting for him to return. They didn't want to make decisions without him and so, in the spring of 1998, he reluctantly returned.

***

Following a thanksgiving dinner in Cagayan de Oro, on 18 November, just days after Des was released, two friends of the Columbans, Fr Bernard (Ben) Maes, a Belgian, and Fr Chito Yanoc, a Filipino, decided to return to the bishop's house in Marawi, where Des had been living.

They took the bus to Marawi, and as soon as Ben approached the gate of the house, two gunmen manhandled him into a waiting car and then quickly made their way towards the edge of the city. The two were former MNLF rebels who wanted to pressurise the government into giving them their share of the twenty million pesos rebel rehabilitation funds.[2]

Ben's superior rang Donie Hogan to find out what steps had been taken to secure Des's release, and Donie told him the procedures, speaking in a flat monotone. He felt himself sinking into a depression. It was as if Des had been taken all over again. He knew Des was the intended target, too, as they had been waiting at his house.

Ben was released after just two days of captivity because the army blocked off the rebels' route into the mountains. It was a tense and frightening period for the religious orders, especially for the foreign missionaries who feared going into Marawi, not knowing what to expect. Some left their parishes and schools during this time.

In Malabang, Rufus resolved to not let fear rule his decisions. He was known among his colleagues for having no fear, although he had in fact been feeling some anxiety for a time. In a letter to Celia Eco at Christmas 1997, he addressed the issue:

> I was only scared two days last week. There is a kidnapper outside of Malabang. I was really afraid Cel [that I would be taken] … it was a great lesson to me of God's ever-caring love for me and never to take it for granted. Des and Ben are pretty okay even if they were kidnapped. The spirit is well in the prelature. It's like one big family. Really God is good. I have an escort, a cousin of Connie's, whenever I go out of Malabang. It's okay, I'm getting used to it and yesterday when I went to Malabang, Cagayan and Iligan I had an escort of 4 soldiers, 4 in civilian clothes. They arrived with me in the car. You just accept these things easily enough as part of the necessary temporary situation. The school and parish are well thank God. I am still alone.[3]

The truth was that Rufus hated having the escorts. He felt they set him apart from the locals, even though he had spent his whole life working to be close with the local people.

In Rufus's letters to Celia, he regularly mentioned the security situation. In February 1998 he wrote:

> We are well T.G. despite all these escorts and security. I see them as an unavoidable temporary necessity. Some of the lads here find them difficult to live with. Also, a question is where does Fr Des stay [upon his return from Ireland]? But for all that he's pretty good, and also Ben.[4]

He was also preoccupied with the work of the missionaries and was conscious of staying on course with his work in the area of dialogue. In the same letter, he addressed this:

> We are very small and few, but there is a great spirit of camaraderie amongst us. And I really admire our diocesan priests. They are very few and there is no money here and it's full of uncertainty, but yet they remain with us here. We are so blessed. Personally I have only been afraid twice over the past three and a half months, and they were very temporary. Just threats. To be without fear is a real grace, and answer to people's prayers.

After Des's kidnapping, the Columbans asked Rufus to be extremely careful and not to go out unless absolutely necessary. He hated this, so he put some caged birds in the dining room to help alleviate the sense of being inside. His loneliness didn't help matters.

In late 1998, however, he finally got the companion he had craved for some time. Fr Dave Cribbin, a Columban from Ireland, joined him in Malabang. Although he had wanted a friend, he found that having a younger priest around made him feel a little insecure. He spoke about this in letters to Celia:

… a young, good-looking Irish priest. He is kind and he
has many gifts and I am very happy. The work is much
lighter. It's also great to have a companion. It is only
now that I have a companion who is younger than me.
Sometimes, I notice myself feeling jealous towards him.
It's terrible – it shows how weak a human being I am. It
will be a very pleasant experience in having him and also
a great challenge for me to accept happily the fact that I
am well into middle age and to be able to let go of the
illusion of eternal youth and perhaps to have a little more
depth. More and more I am happy to be seen as a father
figure to the community here.[5]

He continued his introspective musings and contemplated the
source of his anger, which he felt was a constant source of anxiety
for him:

Thanks, for all the nice things you said vis a vis my loss
of sparkle. All gratefully received though I still think it's
somewhat true. I know that there must be a relation, not
so much to my faith and in my priesthood, but in my
unresolved anger against myself. Ever since I faced this a
year ago, there have been big changes, thanks be to God.
This is one of the insights I received from the retreat. The
one who helped me, the director, kept telling me don't
run, stay with it, the healing will come. That you choose
to stay with it is the work of the spirit and the change will
come unconsciously. So except when I am feeling a bit
fragile, life is great and I sure can relax into and be part
with and of the community, so thanks be to God.[6]

He signed off each letter, as if he was engaging in a conversation:

'It's been lovely chatting to you. I think I'll stop now and have a siesta.'

Rufus soon settled into his new situation with Dave, who had similar interests and hobbies. They both enjoyed keeping their house beautiful despite having no money, and Rufus believed beauty was achievable with the proper use of space. Dave also had a good eye for aesthetics, whether it was in the house, flower arrangements or photography.

One evening, soon after Dave had moved in, they rushed out to get a photo of the sun shining in late afternoon with the green mountain grass underneath. But by the time they arrived, the clouds were blocking the sun. They decided to wait to see if the weather would improve, but as time went on the weather worsened and they soon realised a typhoon was coming. As they walked home, soaked to the skin, Rufus decided that he could either feel sorry for himself, or he could feel incredibly alive with the experience. His personality was naturally positive and he chose to see the joy and goodness in every situation, even to the point where he was soaked by the rain. He smiled as he reflected on one of his favourite sayings from St Irenaeus: 'The glory of God is man fully alive'.

CHAPTER 16

Blessed are the peacemakers, for they will be called sons of God.

Matthew 5:1

Rufus's work as director of Our Lady of Peace High School kept him busy, and he was very engaged with the community. When shootings occurred and people were killed he felt deeply affected by it, and the senseless loss of life weighed heavily on him.

On a Sunday morning in September 1998, he had visited a Christian family whose son, Joel, had been gunned down as he walked home from school for his lunch. Rufus knew that no one would be picked up for the crime, as the perpetrator came from an influential Muslim family, and the boy was a Christian with no standing in the area. As he rode his motorbike to the house, he thought about how difficult the dialogue between Muslims and Christians was, and how he had no stomach for it at times like these. The entire parish was in mourning. He felt heavy and weary.

In an unrelated incident, he had promised to visit a Maranao family later that day, whose seventeen-year-old son had been shot in a feud between two clans. Their daughter attended Our Lady of Peace High School and, although he didn't know the family personally, he offered his condolences as the director of the school.

He couldn't bear to think about more young people being shot in cold blood, simply because of a disagreement between their families that went back years. As he arrived in the area, he met some of the boy's cousins who lived a few houses away. He decided to take a chance.[1] He asked, 'Can nothing be done to end this feud amongst you?'

He was stunned to hear their response. 'Would you help us?'

It was the first time since arriving in the Muslim area eighteen years previously that he had been asked to help out in this type of situation. He felt deeply honoured. The feud had been going on for ten years and had left almost twenty people dead. Rufus continued on to the dead boy's house, through the stunning countryside studded with coconut trees. The beauty of the area contrasted with the wire fences and foxholes that surrounded the houses, protecting them from possible attacks.

The family was very welcoming and friendly. When he spoke to the boy's parents, he said to them, 'At night-time they're your children, during the day in school they're our children.' He continued offering his condolences to the family with a heavy heart, knowing they had just buried a lovely young fellow who was killed for no reason at all.

Before he left, the cousins once again asked him to help them.

'What kind of help?' Rufus asked, wondering if they had something in mind.

'That's up to you,' they responded.

'Alright! I'll go and visit the other side and see what can be done.'

'The one you ask for is Commander Erning.'

Rufus suddenly began to question the wisdom of what he had done. They were looking for peace but were prepared for war, wearing battle fatigues and carrying every weapon imaginable. He realised that a lot of prayer would be needed for this to work. It was going to be extremely difficult and he was worried his Maranao wouldn't be up to scratch, as one wrong word could make the whole thing unravel.

Connie Balindong was delighted and surprised when he told

her what had happened. 'You know,' she said, 'they could not ask another Muslim to do that. It might appear as weakness.'

He was glad of the month-long ceasefire in place between the families as he travelled to the other family involved in the feud a few days later. As he approached the house, he was stopped by a young man carrying a gun.

'Why do you want to see Commander Erning?' he asked, but not in an aggressive manner.

'Oh, it's just a visit,' Rufus responded. The young man agreed, and both men got on the motorbike to find Commander Erning.

In the midst of a cluster of eight houses, Erning sat awaiting his visitor. Rufus was struck by his friendliness as he handed him a coffee.

'Ah, you're the priest from the Our Lady of Peace High School?'

'Yes, that's me.'

He was satisfied when Rufus said it was just a social visit and they talked about how fertile the land around them was, with the trees bending over under the bounty of coconuts. Rufus told Erning and his men that he came from a farm in Ireland, and they questioned him about it. After what seemed like a suitable time, he raised the real reason for his visit: he had spent time with the other family, who were now seeking peace.

'Would you be interested in peace?' Rufus asked, holding his breath. The mood suddenly changed and there was a stillness in the air. Nobody said anything for what seemed like a long time. Then Erning spoke.

'Father, all we're asking for are the seven guns they owe us, and payment of an outstanding debt. We're prepared to settle for that. We are very grateful for your help.'

'So, who would we get to negotiate this?' Rufus queried.

'We would like the Sultan of Barurao,' Erning replied.

Rufus said he would get him, but when he went back to Malabang to meet Connie, she said, 'Oh, no, no, go back to the other side first and make sure they would agree to this person.'

He was relieved when they agreed, so he went to the sultan and told him what was happening. They spoke for a long time, in a friendly fashion, their conversation covering many topics.

'A thousand thanks, my brother, for helping us. You know, both sides are related to me and I'm already working on it. Tell them what you have just told me about how peace has now finally come to Northern Ireland. How they are tired of the killing, and all want peace. I, with the vice-mayor of Matanog, will work on the negotiated settlement. You just keep speaking to them of the benefits of peace, to try and lessen the bitterness.'

Rufus continued to visit both families to resolve their long-standing feud. He was very excited by the role he was playing in this proposed peace settlement, and he wrote to Celia:

> There's already a one-month ceasefire so I went to visit the other side. They received me warmly but I could feel the hatred was deep. But I went back again to the first group, and then last Saturday I visited the local sultan chief, acceptable to both, he said he's working on it but he told me to continue to visit them and speak to them about the fruits of peace and war. My goodness, Cel, what a wonderful mission. So I am trying to pray a bit more. The situation is better after the peace. Imagine after 18 years here to be so trusted, I feel what a role to be given to me.[2]

It became very clear to Rufus that both sides desperately wanted the killings to end. Neither was asking for anything much. He went back to the family who had recently lost their son. 'Who's winning in this conflict?' he asked them.

They responded with silence. They knew everyone had lost.

'Here you are, locked in your area. If you go to Malabang, something might happen to you. Your boys cannot study in high school or college for the same reason. Yet we have here now a real chance for peace, which may not return again. Don't just focus on the faults of the other side. We all have faults. Allah is with us. He wants us to live in peace. Don't squander this opportunity.'

On the first Friday of every month, Rufus visited the sick and the old of the community and he began to ask these people to help him by praying for peace between the families. He believed they had a very real mission and part to play in the peace negotiations, even though they couldn't leave their beds. Everyone he asked agreed to pray without hesitation, even though some of them were lying in bed as a result of being attacked by warring Muslims.

The sultan reported good progress, and there was a further fifteen-day extension to the ceasefire. Rufus noticed they were carrying fewer arms and their 'fighting talk' had somewhat diminished. When he had first started the negotiations, both sides had repeatedly warned him not to trust the other side. After some weeks, they started admitting some of their own failures and looking to themselves to find solutions. The ceasefire was again extended by four days and the sultan confided to Rufus that he believed a settlement was almost agreed upon. Finally, on 17 November 1998, both sides agreed to sign a peace accord in the *municipio* (city hall).

Rufus was proud and excited to have been a part of it. On the way to the signing, he noticed the extra soldiers and police present. Everyone was cautious about an ambush, and the community had seen enough of the wanton violence caused by these families to know that anything was possible and that every precaution should be taken.

Rufus waited in the *municipio* for about an hour and a half before the first side arrived, led by an army jeep with six armed soldiers, followed by a big truck carrying Igid, the leader, and his crew. A big amphibian tank came behind them. They went inside and sat silently smoking, tensely waiting for the other side. They didn't come for another hour, during which time Rufus dispensed with the small talk and sat silently with the Maranao men.

When Erning and his men finally arrived, another 150 people packed into the hall, while their extended family and supporters, numbering in the region of around 100, waited outside.

Nobody looked anyone else in the eye, and there was a lot of tension in the air. The sultan broke the silence and calmed the atmosphere somewhat when he voiced his hopes for the future, where peace would triumph and endure. He brought the main leaders to the front of a long table, where the mayor and vice-mayor of Matanog, two colonels and Rufus were seated, and he then placed the Qur'an, which was covered by a Maranao woven cloth, onto the table.

He unveiled the Qur'an and placed Erning's and Igid's hands on it. Along with their supporters, they swore on the Qur'an to abide by the terms of the agreement. Both were then asked to embrace each other, as a gesture of goodwill. Rufus couldn't help but notice that this gesture was premature, as neither could even look the other in the eye. Despite this, they signed the papers, had a photocall and made speeches.

Rufus was thrilled to be part of it all. It was the pinnacle of his life on mission to date, and he felt really wonderful to have been involved in something so positive. In the next few days, he visited both sides and presented them with a sign he'd had made for them. One side of the sign had 'Abode of War' crossed out, while the other side had written in Arabic *Darussalam*, which means 'abode of peace'. Over the next few weeks and months, Rufus's faith was deepened as he saw how the peace really appeared to have taken effect. Both families started visiting each other socially and, more importantly, the violence and killings stopped.

Rufus told Celia how happy he was to be involved in this process: 'Now three months on, I was out there two days ago only, and the two leaders have met and I would say that arguably it's the greatest thing that happened in my life as a priest, you know.'[3]

CHAPTER 17

Health is the greatest gift, contentment the greatest wealth,
faithfulness the best relationship.

Buddha

Rufus and Dave Cribbin were joined in early 1999 by Fr Jude Genovia, a Filipino Columban priest from Mindanao. Rufus, a very sociable person, was delighted to have another housemate.

'Even if he only stays with us for a few months it will be a blessing. Besides, I like to get the people used to the idea of Columbans being rooted in the Philippines – it's not just a foreign thing.'[1]

His work in the Our Lady of Peace High School kept him busy. He used his role as the director of the school as a way of connecting with the teenagers in the locality, and saw this as a vital component in creating successful and long-lasting relationships. He visited the students frequently and, in their graduation year, he made sure he went to each home to ensure all students were receiving the necessary support.

Noriah Elias was one of his students, although she considered him a friend more than a teacher. She was delighted that a Catholic priest appreciated her culture and religion. When he visited her parents, her mother, who was a traditional Maranao, called him a shark because of his light colouring. She was wary of this foreign, red-haired priest who called to their home, but he soon won her over with his knowledge of Islam and of Maranao culture, and she quickly became close to him.

Noriah visited him in the *convento* and talked about various aspects of life; he had an open house for visitors and they knew an appointment wasn't necessary. She would speak in Maranao and he would reply in English.

He was living Tudtud's version of dialogue, which was to be present in a non-threatening way. Tudtud used to ask, 'Is our presence here good news for the Muslims? The way we live among them, is that good news for them or are they threatened by our presence? Are we relating through our power that we have a lot of money, or that we're in control of projects?'

Rufus was fully versed in Tudtud's theory and vision, but he wanted to be on the front line of the work itself: meeting the Muslims, and being in the school relating to young people and the teachers. He was with the Christian community talking about dialogue while immersing himself in it. His interests weren't confined to his locality, however. He was interested in peace and the peace processes that were taking place around the world. He subscribed to the weekly religious magazine *The Tablet*, and when it arrived he would savour it, reading the issues in chronological order, gradually catching up with news from around the world. He was always interested in reading about any place where there was work for peace – Northern Ireland, Bosnia and Palestine, for example.

He used to say, 'The important thing is to keep people talking with one another. Even if there isn't a whole lot of progress being made, you need to keep people in the negotiations. Keep people talking and working for peace.'

He returned to Waterford for a three-month holiday in April 1999. In July, before he left Ireland, he wrote to Celia, commenting on their friendship:

Funny, as I write this I remember a critique of a book I read yesterday about the relationship between St. Therese of Lisieux and a French missionary called Maurice, and their letters to each other. I quote, 'The letters themselves are the record of a beautiful human love between a man and a woman whose lives were totally given in vowed celibacy to God and to others.' It's beautiful, isn't it?[2]

He clearly saw similarities between this friendship and his relationship with Celia. He treasured his relationships with his friends, and he often used them as a sounding board when he had difficulties in his life. He confided in Celia how he had felt slightly burnt out before going home and that he had lost some of the sparkle in his job.

While on holidays in Ireland, however, Rufus did an eight-day retreat with the Jesuits in Manresa House in Dollymount in Dublin and felt his enthusiasm for his job return. He spoke to the spiritual director on the retreat about his desire to live in a village with Muslims as a simple Christian in the manner Charles de Foucauld had done, and he felt that a clear answer had emerged to him as he prayed. He would have to leave his position as parish priest to do this, but he wanted this idea to become part of a prelature project rather than being a lone ranger expedition. After receiving guidance, he decided he would apply to do this when he returned to the Philippines.

Venus Guibone was also in Ireland during his holiday, working as a lay missionary, so Rufus went to Dalgan Park to meet her. They went to Drogheda for lunch and then visited Newgrange together. He acted as a tour guide, proud of his country's heritage.

Before he returned to the Philippines, he also visited his friend John Robinson in St Jude's parish in Birmingham. He was much-loved by the parishioners there, and they raised £1,500 to send back with him to his parish in Mindanao. John noticed that he seemed particularly radiant, his spirituality shining out of him.[3]

When his holidays ended in July 1999, Rufus returned to Malabang, where he was joined by Fr Paul Glynn. Paul had spent two years in Karomatan and was always interested in working in conflict resolution, as he was inspired by Tudtud's vision for peace. He wanted to contribute to the dialogue, so Des encouraged him to resign as parish priest of Karomatan and to go and live in the Malabang area to learn Maranao. Speaking the Maranao language was a great asset for Muslim–Christian relations, as most Christian Filipinos don't speak the language. When a priest spoke Maranao, the Muslims took him seriously and had great respect for him. Taking the time and effort to learn another language also demonstrated his commitment to better relations.

Rufus told Paul that when he first learned the language he used to insist on speaking it all the time, as he was very proud of himself. If any Filipinos spoke to him in English, he would insist on speaking back to them in their language. He then realised this was driven by his own need to show off that he could speak their language rather than by a desire to communicate effectively, so he adopted a rule of thumb: if somebody spoke to him in English, he would respond in English; if someone spoke in Maranao, he would speak back in that language; he didn't push his own agenda. He made it his business to be transparent, sensitive and caring. He told Paul that dialogue starts with yourself and if you're not communicating with the people around you in their language, then it is hypocrisy to try to enter dialogue between religions.

Paul was a big fan of classical music, something Rufus knew very little about, although he was interested in learning more. He asked Paul if they could hold a musical appreciation night once a week, where they would listen to a piece of music and discuss it. He believed in objective beauty, goodness and aesthetics.

These things were especially important when in Malabang, which was always a precarious place to live, with a lot of violence related to family feuds. Almost every week someone was shot dead. Rufus had a theory that if people could be introduced to beauty it might teach them to seek the way of peace, even when living in a world of violence.

With that in mind he started teaching the final year students the practice of flower arranging known as ikebana. He said it had helped him get in touch with his feminine side, as he had spent most of his life in masculine settings as an athlete.

He admired Japanese flower gardens and went to the Japanese embassy every year to get a copy of their calendar. He appreciated the tidiness and orderliness of the lines, and believed the Japanese to be very neat and orderly. Rufus loved recounting the story of what happened to him years earlier while visiting Japan. He had put his clothes in the laundry basket, including a top that was ripped under the arms, but he liked it because it was comfortable. The Japanese laundry man threw it out because he thought it was garbage.

Paul was in the house after Rufus gave the students their first class in ikebana.

'How did it go, Rufus?' Paul asked.

'Paul, it was great! Would you believe there were a few lads in that class and I know that their fathers are killers, and I know a lot of them could leave school and end up being killers, big lugs of young fellas. The hardest fellas around. And you know what they said at the end of the class? They said, "Father, that was great! Can we do it again next week?"'

Rufus was full of excitement and suggested Paul give a class in classical music as well.

'Keep going with the flower arranging and see how you get on with that first,' Paul replied with a smile.

The musical appreciation nights soon turned into three nights a week and Paul moved into the house with Rufus, Dave Cribbin and Jude Genovia. The town had no electricity, but the house had a generator, which they would put on from 6 p.m. to 9 p.m. each night. Rufus had a room with a string coming in the window by his bed and when they were all lying in bed, he'd shout out, 'Will I turn off the generator?' and if they all said yes he would pull the string and all the lights would go off.

Their daily routine seldom varied. They went to bed very early. From around 4.30 a.m. they would hear the calls to prayer in ten different mosques around the town. The church bells rang at 5 a.m., and they had Mass at 6 a.m. There were no electric fans, so once the morning became hot everyone got up.

The house adjoined the school. The administration rooms were downstairs in the house along with the principal's office. The priests' living quarters were above it, so it was glum and plain, but the flowers helped to cheer the place up and Rufus got the place painted.

Every Tuesday afternoon Rufus would go to Balabagan on his motorbike and come back on Wednesday after his siesta. Soon his housemates joined him on his trips. Dave had his own motorbike, so Jude would ride on the back of one bike and Paul would ride on the back of the other. Balabagan had no electricity either, but it was airier because it was close to the sea. A few priests were living there at the time, including Ben Maes, the Belgian priest who had been kidnapped after Des. Rufus and Ben were close friends and Rufus loved speaking French with him. The fact that Rufus had studied Islamic studies in Louvain in Belgium strengthened their bond.

Rufus was working towards his dream of living a simple life among the Muslims, but first he had to find someone to take his place in the school and parish. His superiors were supportive but said he must have a replacement first. He spoke to the sultans in Malabang, who said that he was accepted among them and there shouldn't be a problem with this move.

After some months, Paul moved on to another parish. In 2000, a Filipino priest called Yrap Nazareno, a member of the Diocese of Bukidnon, moved into the *convento* with Rufus. Dave Cribbin had also left the parish by this time. Yrap came from Malaybalay, which is a one-hour flight north of Cagayan de Oro. He was interested in working as a priest in Muslim areas and had met Des when he first joined the prelature.

In his role as apostolic administrator, Des welcomed him into the prelature and said, 'It's up to you to choose which parish you want to work in. There are six parishes in Marawi.'

Yrap settled on Malabang as it fulfilled the requirements he had in mind: it was close to Marawi and he would be working in areas where Muslims were a majority, but it also gave him the opportunity to work within a Christian setting.

He knew that he was coming to live with a parish priest called Rufus Halley, but he thought Rufus was from the Philippines as the name 'Rufus' sounded very Filipino to him. When Yrap arrived at the *convento*, Juan Cilliado, who worked in the parish, showed Yrap the flower arrangement Rufus had done. Yrap immediately suspected that Rufus might be very effeminate.

Juan must have sensed what Yrap thought, as he said, 'Don't you ever think that Rufus is effeminate! He just loves flower arrangements.'

Yrap said nothing but went for his siesta, wondering what this man who did such beautiful flower arrangements would be like. He soon heard the door open and he went out to introduce himself.

Rufus was wearing a malong. Yrap suddenly became frightened when he saw that Rufus was foreign. A classmate of his had previously served as assistant parish priest with an American and had been treated like a convent boy or a sacristan. It didn't take Rufus long, however, to dispel these fears. He greeted Yrap in fluent Visayan, the Filipino's native language, and Yrap noted that his malong was a very simple, brown-coloured one. Expensive malongs are identified with being wealthy, in the cloth and the way they are cut, but Rufus clearly had chosen a plain one.

He greeted Yrap with an infectious smile, 'Hey, welcome! I'm Rufus. My Filipino name is Popong.'

Because of his age, Yrap should have called him 'father kuya' (older brother), but from the very first moment they met, Rufus insisted that Yrap call him Popong. Yrap felt very awkward with this and it took him about a year to feel at ease calling Rufus by his nickname. But Rufus's behaviour helped him; his actions showed that he never considered himself above anyone else – he was very humble and unassuming, and was so happy when Yrap arrived.

'This is my first time to have a Filipino assistant.' All his previous assistants had been Irish, but he saw it as a step forward that a Filipino would be taking over his role.

Yrap's preconceived ideas about living with foreigners disappeared day by day. The two priests came to a point where they became so close that at every meal they spent about an hour or two just talking and laughing. Friends would say, 'I thought that there were about ten people at the table,' but there were only the two of them.

Rufus and Yrap became very good friends and spent most of their free time together. Both of them liked routine and structure in their lives and they soon settled into a rhythm.

Yrap quickly noticed that Rufus had a deep regard and affection for the poor. Yrap shared his devotion to Charles de

Foucauld. When Yrap was ordained in 1992, he joined a Charles de Foucauld fraternity, the Jesus Caritas fraternity of priests. As part of this he spent at least one hour before the Blessed Sacrament every day in silence. He also spent one day a month in silence and fasting.

Des was part of the same fraternity, and Yrap and Des also became close friends through this association. One day, Yrap asked Des why he wasn't active in it anymore, and Des said it would take him away from the parish too much.

Des was still involved in the Bishop–Ulama Conference meetings, but he often sent Yrap on his behalf. In April, Yrap met Paul Glynn at the meeting in Cagayan de Oro.

'How are you getting on in Malabang?' Paul asked.

'It's going well. I'm using Dave Cribbin's old motorbike, but I have to return it soon, as it is needed in Karomatan for a Father Antonio Estay, who is arriving from Chile.'

'But you need it!' Paul said.

'Yes, but I have to give it back.'

'Don't worry, I'll speak to Des.'

A few days later, Des called Yrap aside and asked if he could find a bike.

'Don't tell anyone, but go and buy a motorbike,' he said as he gave him 50,000 pesos.

Yrap was about to protest, but Des silenced him. 'Just leave it behind in Malabang when you're finished, and the next person can use it.'

Yrap couldn't get over how generous and kind Des was. He was deeply touched by his gentleness. Des always made people feel at home and that everything would be okay.

CHAPTER 18

Mankind must put an end to war, or war
will put an end to mankind.

John F. Kennedy

When Rufus had first moved to Malabang, he began visiting the prisoners in Malabang Provincial Jail every Saturday immediately after breakfast. Most of the prisoners were Muslims. He built up relationships with many and had a very positive attitude towards them. He believed that all people were fundamentally good, no matter what they had done.

People would ask why he visited the jails and he replied that the visits helped restore the prisoners' dignity and self-esteem. He told Yrap they were very lonely in jail.

He carried out many different actions for them. The prisoners would often ask him to bring letters to their family, which he loved to do for them. He would personally deliver the letter. 'The person trusted me and I'll deliver it,' he told Yrap. During Ramadan, Muslim prisoners could only eat once it got dark, but the cooks worked only during the day, so Rufus also arranged food for these prisoners during Ramadan. He asked Bebé, the school treasurer, to send in pandesal bread and old newspapers to the prison. He never brought in goods himself because he didn't want to be identified with money. His philosophy was: 'If you accept me, accept me as I am, not because I have money.'

Rufus also wrote a letter to the provincial governor to find out if the prisoners could receive training in different skills, to make their stay in prison more productive. The governor referred

Rufus to the mayor, who indicated that it wasn't his problem, so Rufus arranged handicraft training for the prisoners himself.

Each Saturday, after visiting the prisoners, he'd travel on his motorbike and pick wild flowers to use during Mass. He made beautiful arrangements from the wild flowers for the house and the church.

Paul Cooney, a priest from Cavan who lived with Rufus for a while during this period, didn't know what to make of this flower arranging and would tease Rufus about it, but Rufus wasn't in the least bit bothered. He would leave the flowers in the living room.

Every Sunday evening at 7.30 p.m. Rufus and Yrap left their house and went to their friend's house to watch a movie. One week, they knew the movie they had chosen to watch was longer than usual, so they decided to go early. At 4 p.m., however, while they were in town, Rufus said he had to visit a student's family. He asked Yrap to wait for him at home, so they could have dinner finished by 6.30 p.m. and then make their way to their friend's house.

Yrap had an hour to kill so he walked around the town for a while. He bumped into a family who invited him in for their daughter's birthday. They weren't having a party because they didn't have any money, but they gave him ice cream, and he spent some time chatting with them.

Suddenly a tropical rain shower started. Yrap watched in dismay as he didn't want to leave during the downpour, but he was conscious of being on time for Rufus. At 6.20 p.m. he couldn't bear to wait any longer, so he grabbed an umbrella and ran back to the *convento*.

Rufus was also caught in the tropical storm, but he was aware that he had asked Yrap to be on time, so at 6 p.m. he put an umbrella over his head, jumped on his motorbike and rode back to the *convento*. When he got there he asked Juan Cilliado if he knew where Yrap was, and Juan simply said that he had seen him at a party in the town.

Rufus ate his dinner quietly and waited until Yrap arrived back at 6.30 p.m., the time they'd originally planned to leave. Yrap could see that Rufus was upset by his late arrival, but there wasn't time to explain where he had gone.

'Eat your dinner quickly,' Rufus said, and he sat watching while Yrap ate in silence.

After a few minutes Rufus said, 'You know if you don't tell anyone where you are going, it's a problem because you might be hurt.' Yrap didn't know how to respond, so he said nothing. Later, as they watched the movie in their friend's house, he couldn't concentrate because he was disturbed that he had upset Rufus.

When it finished they drove home and Yrap couldn't go to bed without talking about what had happened. As Rufus walked past Yrap's bedroom, he stopped him. 'Popong, could we talk for a while? I want to tell you about what happened this evening.'

Rufus opened up to him. 'Yrap, I was worried about you, but I have to admit that I was also jealous because I wasn't invited to the party.'

When Yrap told him there was no party, and explained how the events had unfolded, Rufus's face lit up with understanding. He confided the reason why he was jealous of him.

'You're only three months here, Yrap, and already you're very close to the people.'

Yrap couldn't believe what he was hearing, as Rufus seemed to be so popular and was close to so many people. He began to understand how important it was for Rufus to be fully accepted into the Christian community, just as much as the Muslim community. Yrap felt like crying because Rufus had been so honest and vulnerable.

As he went to sleep, he realised that his time with Rufus was like a formation; he was learning so much from him.

Rufus started to confide in Yrap on a personal level from that point on. There was a very beautiful lady called Dudo, who worked with Bebé. One day, after doing some work in the office, Rufus said to Yrap, 'You seem to be very good with the opposite sex.' He paused for a moment. 'She's beautiful. I would not trust myself alone in a room with her.'

Yrap just smiled and accepted the compliment, although he was thinking, 'If only you knew.' Yrap struggled with his feelings towards women all the time, but he knew it was natural and something that would always be a challenge for him.

He was humbled by Rufus's truthfulness, which had no pretences or presumptions at all. When he came home from a holiday in Ireland one time, he first gave a *pasalubong* to Yrap, then to Dudo.[1] He wasn't afraid to be open with his emotions around people. He had no problem seeking professional help when he struggled and put this into practice by trying to help the people around him.

'You know Yrap, when I retire, I plan to engage in work to help the priests in the psycho-emotional parts of life. There are some people who are in need of help. If I had the opportunity to choose what I could do when I leave Malabang, I'd choose to work in this area.'

Yrap watched as Rufus regularly performed simple acts of kindness. He often tried to hide it when he gave things to people. He asked Yrap to ask Bebé to give two kilos of rice to a poor woman, and Rufus said he would then give Bebé the money. One day, while in Cagayan de Oro, Rufus said, 'Let's buy a watch. I know someone who needs a present.' They visited a very poor family and gave the watch to the daughter, who was celebrating her birthday.

During the celebration of Saint Roque's fiesta on 16 August, Rufus suggested they move around and visit houses in the community. 'Let's go around to the poor families. Now is the perfect time to visit them because they will have prepared meals and it's the only time they won't be embarrassed to see us because they will have something to offer.'

As part of the fiesta in Malabang, everyone prepared special food and invited neighbours and friends to visit them. They created two tables; one for Muslims and one for Christians. The Christians ate *lechón* – pig stuffed with bamboo as big as arms and roasted outside over charcoal until the skin became brittle. They also served spaghetti and *humba* – pork cooked in vinegar and sauce. For sweets they served *bico*, a type of rice pudding, and *suman*, rice pudding rolled in banana leaves.

Yrap and Rufus made it to ten houses together, eating and drinking in each one. Then Rufus could take no more: 'Oh no, Yrap, I have to give up. I can't eat another thing.'

Yrap drove him home and then visited the remaining families on his own.

Yrap felt he was like an apprentice to someone who embodied the word 'Christian'. But the entire parish didn't feel this way and some of the parishioners started to show a preference for other priests, which deeply hurt and surprised Rufus.

Some of the parishioners would say to Yrap, 'We want David Cribbin to say the Mass because he is young.' Many of them didn't accept Rufus; they said he loved the Muslims more than them and that he spent more time with them.

When Yrap would give homilies at Mass, he often spoke about how the Bible said love your enemies. He would then use Rufus's friendship with the Muslims as an example of this practice being brought to life.

***

The parishioners were soon distracted from the minute details of life by an upsurge of violence in the region. On 25 February 2000, forty-four people were killed when two home-made bombs exploded on two passenger buses being ferried from Kolambugan to Ozamiz.[2] The *Lady Mediatrix* ferry, which carried the two Super Five buses, was about twenty metres across Panguil Bay when the bombs went off.[3] The explosions started a fire and created a panic on board. Many of the passengers jumped overboard, even the ones who couldn't swim.

These attacks were part of a series of bombings. At exactly the same time, a bomb went off on a Super Five bus in the nearby town of Rizal, with five people killed in that explosion. Many people were also badly injured during the explosion, suffering third degree burns.[4]

Because Ozamiz was predominantly a Christian city, most people immediately suspected that the MILF was behind the bombings. There was a tenuous peace agreement between the military and the MILF at the time; it was agreed that if the military would leave the MILF alone in their camps, the MILF wouldn't come out of the mountains and engage in kidnappings and murder.

Some people speculated that the military was involved in the bombing, so they would have an excuse to start a war. The military loved times of war because the Americans had, in the past, sent them arms, which they would then, in some cases, sell to the rebels.

The ordinary people in Ozamiz reacted very badly to the bombings and started to blame every Muslim in the area for the attacks. Muslims became targets in the city; people were mugged and stones were thrown at the mosques.

Rufus was in the Columban house in Ozamiz at the time. He was horrified at what he saw happening, so he went to the mosque on behalf of the Christian population. He said most Christians didn't agree with what was happening and he wanted to apologise. He also went on local radio, condemning the attacks against the ordinary Muslim people.

It turned out that Muslim rebels had nothing to do with the explosions. It was later revealed that criminals were running a protection racket against the bus company, Super Five, and the owner of the company had refused to pay protection money. He had been subjected to numerous threats, but this was the first act of violence. However, unaware of the true background, the military, under President Joseph Estrada's rule, waged an all-out war on the MILF.[5]

On 15 March 2000, a combat patrol of the Philippine army came across MILF guerrillas in Kauswagan and killed two of these rebels. The MILF's retaliation was swift. The following day, 700 rebels attacked nine army detachments in Lanao del Norte. Fighting spread to central and northern Mindanao. The MILF surrounded the town hall in Kauswagan and took 400 residents hostage. They closed down the road outside with boulders and coconut trees so no one could come in or out, causing a lot of disruption to Mindanao's business and agricultural communities.[6] The military sent in their tanks and placed a siege on the town.

President Joseph 'Erap' Estrada (who was a former actor in *Rambo*-type movies) decided to play it hard. He said he would unleash the dogs of war onto the MILF and started a targeted campaign.

This campaign culminated in the military overrunning the MILF's headquarters, Camp Abubakar in Barira, Maguindanao. President Estrada flew from Manila to Kauswagan in a helicopter with roast pig and San Miguel beer, which showed complete contempt to all Muslims. Then the army blew up the mosque in the camp.

After that the military would terrorise the people in the area, particularly the Muslims. They would go to people's houses and tell them to evacuate because their lives were under threat. They looted the houses, driving off with their jeepneys stuffed with statues, fridges, brassware – anything valuable at all.

Rufus was particularly upset by these actions and wrote to the cardinal, asking him to campaign to stop the war. Rufus eventually decided that he could take a stand by refusing to say Mass for the military. On 22 June, he sent a letter to Lt Colonel Greg Catapang, which was published in the *Philippines Today* newspaper:

> Some of your men have come inquiring about having the Eucharist with you tomorrow. I have always enjoyed going there to say Mass, and have found the welcome warm and sincere. However, I feel that it would not be appropriate on my part to say Mass there at the moment. I share the sentiments of my religious superiors here in Mindanao in being opposed to this conflict. I do appreciate your position of being under your superiors in Manila.
>
> So while the present policy of the government is operative, I feel it would be better to postpone the Eucharist at the camp until such time as both sides lay aside their arms, sit down, and dialogue about their problems.
>
> I thank you for your kind understanding, and please accept my kindest regards.[7]

The Colonel, however, did not understand and told the newspaper that he was 'slighted' when Rufus refused to bless his men before they went into battle.

'My soldiers and I were appalled at Fr Halley's decision because we badly needed his blessings, because each of us who goes to war will never know if we ever come back alive. And as Christians and Catholics, our inclination to be nearer our God is pronounced during times of utmost uncertainties like war,' he said.[8]

Rufus was asked to reconsider his position, but he said he was clear in his letter. Dave Cribbin took over the monthly Mass and celebrated the Eucharist with the soldiers in Rufus's place.

Not all Catholics were happy with Rufus's stance, and some wrote letters to the newspapers saying that he should be deported. Yrap had to console many families, who were worried that Rufus may in fact be deported. In the end he was allowed to maintain his position.

After many months of violence, dialogue began to take place between the government and the MILF. On 5 October 2000, 669 MILF members surrendered to President Estrada in Cagayan de Oro. On 29 December, a further 855 rebels surrendered, and on 14 March 2001, 931 surrendered to Estrada's successor, President Gloria Macapagal Arroyo, handing over firearms, rocket-propelled grenades, machine guns, mortars and pump boats.[9]

For now, at least, the war was over.

CHAPTER 19

Be on your guard; stand firm in the faith;
be courageous; be strong.

Corinthians 16:13

The Columbans were social activists and worked to improve their communities where possible. One scheme suggested by Fr Paul Cooney involved setting up a Grameen bank, which was a model based on micro-finance, designed to give money to impoverished people. Basically, it gave small loans without seeking collateral.

Rufus set up a branch in Malabang and asked a local woman to run it on his behalf. He decided, however, not to have an auditor; there were no checks and balances and no internal reports. Rufus drove this woman around on his motorbike every Wednesday to collect payments, forgoing his daily siesta. He had great faith in people and trusted everyone to do the right thing, to the point where he could be naïve.

As part of the Grameen bank, they compiled yearly accounts and, in December 2000, when Bebé, Rufus and an accountant audited the books, they found 250,000 pesos unaccounted for. There was no money in the bank. Rufus returned home to the *convento*, devastated. 'Yrap, this is betrayal,' he declared.

This money had not been stolen in one day. Rufus had sacrificed so much to help the local people, and the woman who administered the accounts had looked him in the eye while she betrayed him.

Although he was a gentle person, he also believed strongly in justice and honesty. He was overcome by the betrayal and became so angry he went to her house and took all her valuables. Then he brought her to a lawyer and made her promise that even if she couldn't give it all back at once, she should pay 500 pesos a week. Even though Rufus was trusting, he could be strong when he needed to be. Living in a place where violence and anger were ever-present had made him decisive.

Violence and the threat of violence was always an undercurrent for the missionaries living in Malabang. Every time Yrap and Rufus sat down to a meal, they had the previous day's newspaper in front of them. Their neighbour got the daily paper delivered to his house in the evening, and the next day at 6 a.m. he'd drop it in to Rufus and Yrap. As they ate their breakfast and read the paper, the conversation sometimes came around to the threat of further kidnappings.

'You are so brave to stay here, Popong,' Yrap said to him one evening. 'Are you not afraid of being kidnapped?'

'I'm not brave, Yrap! I am afraid sometimes, but when I pray during my hour before the Blessed Sacrament, I get peace and I get courage. The violence and the greed sicken me. I'll tell you something, if I was kidnapped, I would not give them one peso. I wouldn't want my family or the church to give them any money. I would hate to think they would get money because of me, because if that happened it would just go on and on and they would think that it's a great and easy way to make money. I would show them that not everyone is afraid of their guns.'

Yrap looked on in astonishment at the conviction of this foreign priest sitting in front of him. Rufus radiated confidence and peace, but Yrap knew it wasn't always easy to have the courage of one's convictions, and he hoped that Rufus's would never be tested.

Rufus echoed these sentiments in a letter he wrote to Celia one morning while Yrap read the daily paper:

Yrap is sitting opposite me reading the paper, he's well and off tomorrow for his seminary homecoming. He's still here thank God and his Bishop says he can stay till his scholarship money arrives. For his sake I hope it comes soon or not till next year. It's not easy to start mid-year in another country and culture.

As regards myself I am great thank God, and I settled down immediately here. Ever since I came back there has been strong warning about the Abu Sayyaf and their plan to kidnap either me or a Chinese businessman. But I feel that it's not true as I haven't heard about it from my Muslim friends. I don't know. Of course there is fear when I listen to it but it doesn't last long. After 15 minutes in front of God it disappears. That's a gift thanks be to God.[1]

Writing to his brother Gerry in March 2001, he addressed his burning desire to live simply among the Muslims in his locality:

I have just done my week's retreat and I really feel this call to live in a Muslim village. I tried to resign [as parish priest] two years ago, but Des, while liking the idea, put it on the back-burner. Since the yen has come back again I'll give a stronger push this time. Now, I live in a conven-to with another priest (a Diocesan, and grand chap) here in the town (80% Muslim). Living in the barrio would mean more simple living while relying much more on my neighbours – 100% Muslim and they are amenable to the idea too.[2]

Rufus was planning on spending seven weeks in Ireland that summer. He told Gerry that he was particularly conscious of spending more time with their mother, as he figured she was getting old and mightn't have much time left.

***

Des had gone back to Ireland in October 2000 for a sabbatical break, during which time he did a three-month Clinical Pastoral Education course at St Vincent's Hospital in Dublin. He wanted to lead spiritual retreats for individuals, and while doing the course in St Vincent's he focused on developing listening and understanding skills. He then went to St Beuno's Jesuit Spirituality Centre in Wales to do a ten-week course on training for spiritual directors.

In June 2001, he got a phone call from Rufus to say that he was back in Ireland and he'd love to meet up. They had lunch in Carlow and spent many hours discussing what was happening in the Philippines.

Rufus brought Des up to date on Bishop Edwin de la Peña, who had taken over Des's position of apostolic administrator of Marawi. As they spoke, Des noticed the difference in attitude between Rufus and himself. Rufus didn't appear to see any danger in the work he was doing.

'Des, you know people are always trying to warn me, or trying to say to me you shouldn't do this or you shouldn't do that. But I have great belief. People are essentially very good.'

Des looked at his friend and contemplated his words. He wanted to believe it was true, but his own experiences had taught him there are people who also have badness in them.

'I really feel the calling to go and live amongst the Muslims, like their brother. It's getting stronger all the time, but I really don't want to be like a "lone ranger" doing it. I've done enough of that, and I don't want to isolate myself from the church,' Rufus confided.

Des empathised with Rufus, and in many ways he felt that he was in a similar position. He had also recently felt a strong calling – to start working in retreats and leave the parish life behind. Rufus's superiors were telling him they still needed somebody in the parish and school, and he couldn't leave until his replacement was found, so he reluctantly stayed, but all the time he was making plans for when he could leave.

A week later, Rufus travelled to Tullamore to have lunch with Venus, who was now working as a lay missionary there. He came straight from the dentist but was able to enjoy the Filipino-style rice that Venus cooked for them. He then pulled jasmine tea leaves from his shirt pocket, which he had brought for her all the way from the Philippines.

It was as if no time had elapsed between them, as they spoke frankly to one another. Rufus noted how times had changed, with Filipino missionaries now needed in Ireland. He gave her news from her native country and spoke in particular of his involvement with Tabang Mindanao (which means Help Mindanao in Visayan), a humanitarian project formed by NGOs, media companies, private businesses and the Catholic Church, in partnership with the government and the military. Tabang Mindanao was set up to address hunger and to help victims of conflict in Mindanao. He showed her photos of activities with displaced residents in the Cotabato, Maguindanao and Lanao areas during President Estrada's all-out war campaign against 'Muslim terrorists'.

'I can't understand how things were allowed to get so bad. It's sad how the situation was dealt with,' he said.

He soon came back to a story of hope, though, and told her about the peace agreement he brokered between the two warring families, showing her photos of them. He was so enthused about this experience, and the feeling that after all these years something like this could happen. 'I am just so grateful that it could happen, and that I was able to play some small part in it.'

When Venus later reflected on the conversation, she was struck in particular by what he said next.

'Some people have told me I may be the target of kidnap attacks by Abu Sayyaf members, Venus. It makes me so angry to think about being kidnapped,' he said, sighing heavily, and she noted that he looked sad and frustrated.

He then switched to Visayan to get his point across more strongly. 'I'd rather die than be kidnapped. It is such an unjust act, making money by kidnapping somebody.'

Venus was very struck by his strong sentiments.

After several hours of reminiscing and exchanging news, Venus went as far as the main Tullamore road with Rufus, and there she bid him goodbye. He gave her a long kiss on the cheek, which was not typical of him, and as she watched him drive away, she felt very nostalgic because she knew it would be some time before she would see him again.

A few weeks later, Gerry drove him to the airport. He knew Rufus was sometimes lonely, and they ended up having a deep conversation.

'Is there a God, Rufus? Do you ever have any doubts?'

Rufus replied in a jovial voice without a second's hesitation: 'None at all. I'm more certain now than ever before of my beliefs. The last fifteen years have been the happiest of my life. I've never been closer to the man above.'

At the airport, Rufus embraced his brother in his customary bear hug and wished him well, saying he would see him on his next trip. Gerry watched his brother walk away, grateful that he was content in his mission.

***

Rufus arrived back in the Philippines on 11 July 2001, and after landing in Manila, he visited Celia at the Little Sisters house in Mandaluyong. He stayed for most of the day with her and at about 3 p.m. he said he'd like to take a rest because he was going to visit Fr Kevin McHugh later.

'Do you have time to visit some of the sisters in the other house?' Celia asked hopefully, as two of her colleagues who were based in their house in Quezon city in another part of Manila wanted to talk to him.

'Of course, let's go,' he replied cheerfully, so they made their way there together.

On the way, he spoke once more about his desire to live among the Muslims in the way that Charles de Foucauld did. It was foremost on his mind, and he said it frequently to all his friends. He was adamant he didn't want to work completely alone, however. He still wanted to be part of the Columban family while he had made major progress in terms of his aim of living more fully among the Muslim community.

'I've found a place to live, Cel. Would you believe it's in Matanog, the place where I negotiated the settlement for peace between the two Maranao clans?'

'What about your security?'

'The leader of the place assured me they would take care of me. Connie said they would lay down their life to protect me, and I feel very confident.'

He reiterated this confidence in a letter to his sister, Evelyn, around this time:

> Living here in this area precludes taking life for granted. The people are quite volatile and life, while being precious, can at times appear cheap; it's quite violent. And on my return I was told that the Abu Sayyaf kidnappers were

in town. Ben – a Belgian missionary in the next town – was warned almost not to leave the house. Please God they are just rumours, which tend to proliferate in times of uncertainty. The great news is I'm not afraid! And this is [a] pure gift. So, I just get on with it, while believing myself to be totally in His hands.[3]

He speculated with Celia about what type of house he might live in, and assumed it would be something like the one belonging to the Little Sisters in Quezon city, a very simple structure.

'I want it to be as simple as possible, Cel, but I would need my own room,' he continued. Privacy was very important to him. He went on to say that it would have to be a place where people come on Sunday and a place for prayer, which was always of utmost importance to him.

After meeting with the other Little Sisters, Rufus decided to leave, and Celia went a little of the way with him in the jeepney. She had asked him the last time they spoke on the phone not to hug her goodbye the next time they met, as she was always embarrassed when people saw them hug.

When they were saying their goodbyes, Rufus was feeling very uncomfortable because he wanted to hug her. He didn't know what to do, when suddenly Celia remembered a previous conversation when he had asked her when she was going to touch his face and, on impulse, she put her hand on his cheek. Her heart skipped a little when she saw his smile light up his face, and she felt overwhelmed with love and gratitude for her friend, who had been her spiritual partner throughout her adult life. She suddenly understood how they had been drawn together in their spiritual search, but as they grew more comfortable with their spirituality, they were able to become more human in their expressions of friendship. She then touched him on his hand and said goodbye.

***

When Yrap first moved to Marawi, his original agreement with the bishop was that he would stay only for a year and then leave to study Islam, as he had applied for a scholarship to pursue this academic aim. As his year approached an end, Yrap became aware that he was becoming more interested in Muslim–Christian relations, and he spent a lot of time talking to Rufus about the best way to improve relationships between the two communities. Rufus advised him that he needed to stay in the region longer, so he could learn Maranao.

'If you stay for another year, Yrap, I'll help you with your studies,' Rufus said.

In July 2001, Yrap approached his bishop, Honesto Pacana, to receive permission to remain another year in Malabang. The bishop didn't give his consent, however, and said he could stay for just three more months to learn the language. Yrap was upset and decided to leave rather than pretend he could learn a language in three months.

When Rufus returned from Ireland, he heard the news of Yrap's imminent departure and said, 'How about the possibility of you staying? We'll send two jeepneys to persuade the bishop.'

'No, no. I know the bishop. He'll just dig his heels in,' Yrap replied dejectedly, but Rufus wouldn't accept this as an answer. He went on his bike from Malabang to Cagayan de Oro, which was a five-hour ride, and then travelled for an hour on a bus to speak to Yrap's bishop face to face.

Bishop Pacana was cordial to Rufus, and ultimately met him halfway. 'He has already applied for a scholarship. If it should come, he should take it, but if not, then it's up to him where he lives.'

Rufus rushed back to share the news, as he felt certain that Yrap wouldn't get the scholarship in time for the coming academic year, which meant he could stay in Malabang. When they spoke, he advised him to do Islamic studies in Birmingham when he did ultimately gain his scholarship, but told him not to bother studying Arabic and that Maranao would prove much more useful in the context they were working in. Satisfied that he had at least another year in Malabang, Yrap started travelling around the community with Rufus, trying to pick up as much Maranao as he could.

**

One Sunday morning a few weeks later, Rufus and Yrap were eating breakfast after the first Mass when three young Maranaos started stealing candles from the church. Rufus flared up and became furious instantly, showing his red-haired fiery roots. Yrap had never seen him get so exercised about anything before; he was usually very easy-going. However, on this occasion he jumped out of his chair and ran towards the church so he could drag the boys away. He started shouting at them in Maranao, and although Yrap couldn't understand what he was saying, by his volume and tone he knew the boys were receiving a severe dressing down.

Bebé lived with her family next door to the church, where they ran a restaurant and bakery. During this altercation, some of her children were peeping out the window because Rufus's voice was so loud.

The boys answered back in their native tongue, and it was obvious that they fought back.

Eventually Rufus came back to the table, took a deep breath and said, 'Ha!' He paused for a minute before continuing. 'I think I over-reacted, Yrap.' He seemed to realise he shouldn't have gotten so upset, and then he continued his meal.

Later that day he bought his favourite fruit – jackfruit – and had it with his lunch. During lunch he said to Yrap, 'Do you remember the boys I scolded in the church?'

'Yes.'

'I passed by them on the road. One of the kids pointed his finger at me as if he was pulling a trigger and said, "You're dead, my friend."'

Yrap didn't know what to say, but he assured Rufus he wouldn't be killed because he had scolded some children.

The following morning, a Monday, Yrap had time to linger over breakfast with Rufus as he was going to Cagayan de Oro for the feast of St Augustine and his driver was late. When the priests needed to travel somewhere they always used the same vehicle (named 'Suki') and the same driver for security purposes.

Rufus and Yrap were in the middle of a good chat when Bebé arrived. She often sat at the table with them while they ate. In this instance she told them she was going away for a few days to visit her son. The conversation then came around to the behaviour of the children the previous day.

Bebé said, 'Perhaps, Father, if the Muslims, the Maranaos, were more educated they would not behave like this; they would be more civil and more loving.'

'No, no Bebé! If you get high education you will be more crooked, but I know you will not become a good person because of education,' Rufus replied. 'I know lots of people at home who have no education, but they really are very nice and good, good people.'

Yrap was listening to them and found that he agreed with Bebé.

'Perhaps, Popong, what Bebé is saying is that if you get a good education and good exposure you will not act – the Maranao – would not act the way they do in Malabang.'

There were almost daily killings in Malabang and most of these were among the Maranao community. Rufus was very, very strong and he defended his position. Yrap found that he resented Rufus's opinion.

'Why are you defending these people? Every time I hear from Christians they are being mistreated by the Muslims. I sympathise with them.'

Rufus poured himself another coffee and didn't reply. Yrap then fell silent and started to process his own feelings. By the time breakfast was finished he had gotten over his resentment. Yrap really respected Rufus's point of view because of his experience and the goodness of his heart.

Who am I to question his opinion? he thought. He was barely a year in his position and realised he shouldn't be insisting on his own point of view.

When the car finally arrived, they hugged each other goodbye, and Rufus said, 'Good luck, Yrap. See you soon!'

It would be the last time Yrap would see him alive.

***

Rufus was a security nightmare, insofar as he liked to stick to a certain routine. For years, on his day off every Tuesday, he would take his motorbike and visit friends in neighbouring Balabagan before returning to Malabang on Wednesday. This week, however, he changed his routine slightly and stayed overnight in Balabagan on Monday as he had promised to marry a poor Catholic couple in a quiet, private ceremony in the Our Lady of Peace parish church at 4 p.m. on 28 August 2001.

On Tuesday, he arose at his usual time of 5.30 a.m. and spent an hour in front of the Blessed Sacrament. He then spent the day with Ben Maes, and at about 3.40 p.m. he mounted his motorbike, put on his gloves, and his soft, white hat to protect his head from the sun. He said goodbye in his usual manner, 'Until next week, lads!' and waved.[4]

It was a typical summer's evening in the tropics; balmy and dusty, and Rufus rode his bike as he usually did – at a steady pace, enjoying his surroundings. When he approached the Diamaru Elementary School in Malabang, at about 4.30 p.m., a Second World War military truck was parked outside, blocking the road. As Rufus slowed, six armed men jumped out and surrounded him.

A brief conversation took place between the priest and the men, during which he tried to reason with them. The men spoke Maranao, and Rufus is likely to have asked them to consider what they were doing.

They manhandled him, forcing him off his bike and tried to drag him into their truck. Rufus resisted fiercely. He managed to wrench himself free and started to run for his life.

One of the men shot Rufus with an M-16 as he tried to escape. The first bullet went into the back of his knee, and although Rufus stumbled, he kept running. The next shot landed in his right buttock, and Rufus fell to the ground.

Things had not gone according to plan for the would-be kidnappers, and they now panicked as they realised Rufus could identify them. One of the would-be abductors strode over to the injured missionary and shot four more bullets into his body. Rufus instinctively lifted his hand to protect his head. The final bullet went straight through his hand and into his face. It was at such a close range that it blew his dentures out, and his glasses fell off.

With that, Rufus's life ended, his blood slowly seeping into the Philippine soil. The man who had dedicated his life to helping people was given a most horrific death.

CHAPTER 20

Those who are closest to Allah's heart are those who
walk gently on the earth, and when the ignorant
address them as 'fool' they reply 'peace'.

Passage from the Holy Qur'an

The first person at the scene was a teacher from Cotabato who taught in the public school. She was riding in a passenger van, when somebody told her a priest had been shot dead. She cautiously walked over to where Rufus lay, about ten metres from his motorcycle. One of his sandals had fallen off. She cried out as she recognised him immediately as Popong, then hurried to the *convento* to break the news. Juan Cilliado, who lived in the basement of the *convento*, was the first person she found.

By the time Juan got to the scene, Choi, a Catholic lady from the parish, was guarding the body with the police. All the teachers were there, howling with grief. The police wouldn't let anyone near the body, but Juan ran past them to get to his friend. Rufus's brain was scattered everywhere, so Juan picked up Rufus's hat from the ground and gathered up every part he could see. His instinct was to put him back together; it seemed disrespectful to have his body in pieces.

The military wouldn't let anyone move the body because they wanted to make a sketch for their report. Juan contacted a photographer to capture the scene more quickly. Once this was done, they moved his body into the little house next to the church, where Rufus and Yrap used to eat their meals.

***

Yrap was in Cagayan de Oro for a fiesta and an alumni homecoming. On the Tuesday, he went to the Columban house and stayed for lunch. At 5 p.m. he answered the phone to one of his parishioners, Thomas, who didn't spend time on pleasantries.

'Popong has been ambushed.'

'Don't make a joke about that,' Yrap admonished him.

'No, it's true. I've seen him. He's been shot dead and he's already at the church,' Thomas continued.

Yrap felt his knees begin to buckle, so he steadied himself against the wall. He could hardly believe what he'd just heard, yet part of him knew it must be true. He was suddenly overwhelmed by grief and anger, and ran out to the grounds of the house, not knowing what to do.

Yrap remembered Rufus being threatened by the children and he started screaming and crying, 'Why? Why did they have to do that? Why did you have to kill him for scolding you? Why?'

He just couldn't understand how something like this could have happened.

About thirty minutes later, Thomas called again and told Yrap that Rufus had been travelling from Balabagan. On his way home there was an attempted abduction and he was shot dead. It was only then that Yrap realised his death had nothing to do with the kids.

Thomas told him that plans for Rufus's burial had already been made, and they had sent for an embalmer from Cotobato, but it would take some time as there was no transport to Malabang that day.

Yrap rang Fr Colm McKeating, the Columban regional director, and made plans to travel with him to Malabang the following morning. He spent the rest of the evening trying to come to terms with the news. He alternated between extreme shock and numbness. He experienced the grief so badly that he felt like a man possessed. He couldn't stop crying; he simply couldn't accept that his friend and mentor was gone.

***

Gerry Halley was sitting in his office on Georges Street in Waterford when his phone rang. The caller identified himself as Fr Hopkins, the local priest, and in a grave voice he said, 'Hello, Gerry. I want to see you.'

Gerry was always glad to hear from Fr Hopkins and greeted him cordially. 'That's no problem, Father. When would you like to meet?'

'Straight away.'

'I can't, I'm afraid I'm about to go into a meeting.'

'I have very bad news, Gerry. I have to see you urgently.'

Gerry paused for a split second, a thousand thoughts racing through his head. He kept his voice steady as he asked, 'What is it?'

'It's Rufus.'

A cold hand gripped the solicitor's heart as he thought of his older brother. He could hear the anguish in the priest's voice on the other end of the line as he struggled to find the right words.

'What is it?' Gerry asked again, softly.

'He's been murdered in Mindanao,' Fr Hopkins said in a broken tone. 'I'm so sorry, Gerry.'

Gerry hung up, feeling completely numb. He couldn't take in the enormity of the priest's words. He went to find his brother Emmet, who ran the family's legal firm with him. Still in a daze and not fully comprehending what he was saying, the words somehow stumbled out that their brother had been violently killed on the other side of the world. Emmet was horrified and immediately struck with grief. They decided they should gather the remaining three brothers together to break the news.

Gerry then rang his wife, Debbie, who had always been very close to Rufus, and one by one they informed their own family.

Their mother, Imelda, was visiting their sister, Evelyn, in Canada, so Gerry rang Evelyn and told her as gently as he could. Evelyn asked what seemed like hundreds of questions, but Gerry had no answers. All he knew was that Rufus was dead. That much was certain, it seemed.

Rufus had always thought of the Columbans as his other family, so Gerry let them handle all the arrangements surrounding the funeral. He knew there was a question as to whether he would be buried in Malabang; and that the Columbans couldn't guarantee the safety of the Halley family if they went there. Because of the tropical heat, there was also the question of getting Rufus's remains embalmed as quickly as possible, but Gerry knew these challenges were being handled.

Really what he struggled with in the immediate aftermath was accepting the news of his older brother's murder.

***

Rufus was killed on the feast day of St Augustine, 28 August 2001. Paul Glynn was celebrating the feast in the wooden chapel in Sugod, which is a tiny *barrio* about an hour's walk from where he lived in Sigayan. There are many small villages in the Philippines that don't have priests living there permanently, so he did a few baptisms while he was there. It was customary on the island to have a baptism on a feast day. He stayed in the village until the intense heat had left the air, and then he walked home to his wooden house, where he lived with two Maranao students – Ali and Lucman.

They had dinner and relaxed. At 7 p.m. a vehicle arrived and Ali said, 'It's Fr Nilo,' because he saw the car belonged to the parish house in Karomatan. Paul immediately knew something was wrong because people didn't normally travel that road at night due to the bandits. It wasn't Nilo who got out of the car, however, but a good friend of Paul's, Fred. Ali asked him why he was there.

'Bad news,' Fred replied, and Paul instantly thought of his mother and father. However, Fred said, 'Popong has been shot.'

Paul's initial reaction was one of disbelief. 'Fred, that's not funny,' Paul said. 'Popong hasn't been shot.'

'He's been shot dead in Malabang.'

'Will you stop that nonsense? Who would want to kill Popong?'

'Paul, I'm telling the truth.'

Paul simply couldn't believe it. 'Are you sure, Fred? Who would want to kill Popong? He has no enemies.'

'Paul, he was shot; they don't know who shot him, but he was shot. He was driving his motorbike and he was shot,' Fred repeated.

Two neighbours of Fred, Lucy and Celia, had come with him, and they sat in the car as Fred broke the news. Lucy shouted out, 'Fred, did they steal the motorbike?'

Paul didn't know what to do with his emotions and he reacted with anger. 'Why are you worried about the bike? It's Rufus we're worried about.'

'Were they trying to kidnap him or steal the motorbike?' she clarified. Paul said he hadn't thought of that and later apologised to her.

Fred answered her question. 'No, the motorbike was lying at the side of the road. They weren't trying to steal the motorbike, it was something more serious.'

He turned to Paul. 'You need to come with me to Karomatan. Pat Baker is in charge in Ozamiz and he wants you to phone him as soon as possible.'

Paul got into the jeep immediately and they drove to nearby Karomatan. He kept asking the whole way, 'Why would anyone want to kill Popong?'

Nobody had any answers.

When they got to Karomatan there was no landline in the town and no proper coverage for mobile phones. The only way to get coverage was to go down to the seashore, so at 8.30 p.m. Paul stood in about two inches of water with the sea wetting his shoes. As he felt the waves lap around his feet, he was struck by the contrast between the mundane and the important. *This is important; it doesn't matter if my shoes get wet*, he thought. Eventually he got through to Pat Baker, the Columban superior in Mindanao, who told him there was no priest in Malabang at the moment because Yrap was in Cagayan de Oro, attending a class reunion.

Baker admitted, 'We're very anxious. Rufus has been killed. We feel a Columban should be there as soon as possible. Will you go?'

Paul said he'd go first thing in the morning.

'You'll be the first down there; can you make arrangements for his funeral?'

A worrying thought struck Paul. 'I'm sorry for saying this, Pat, and I hope it doesn't alarm you, but we mightn't have to make any arrangements for the funeral. That's a Muslim area and they may have buried him in their custom, which is to bury someone on the day they die.'

'Oh, I didn't think of that.'

Paul planned to get a boat to Malabang the next morning, as there was no road between Karomatan and Malabang at the time, but his friends advised him against travelling.

'You don't know why Popong was killed,' Lucy urged him. 'You might arrive at the pier and someone might try to shoot you.'

Pat Baker then phoned Paul back to say there'd been a change of plan. The regional director of the Philippines, Colm McKeating, was going to travel down to Iligan the next day and the CICM Fathers would send a vehicle to Iligan to collect Paul, Yrap and Colm to bring them to Malabang.

Fred and Paul stayed up talking all night, and at 3 a.m., Fred drove Paul to the Mercy Sisters' headquarters in Camague in Iligan city, where they met Yrap and Colm.

At 10.45 a.m. they travelled very quietly to Malabang in an FX Toyota with darkened windows, each of them feeling numb and lost. No one knew what to expect when they arrived.

Malabang was about three hours in a car from Iligan, and there were many military checkpoints along the way. The driver drove fast and carelessly, and nearly crashed into the barriers of two checkpoints. At one of the checkpoints the policeman said, 'You look like you're in a hurry. Did you not see that?'

Paul found himself once again getting annoyed; this time with the driver. He couldn't contain his emotions at all. Yrap was in a similar situation, but his grief manifested itself in the tears that wouldn't stop flowing.

When they arrived in Malabang, they didn't know where they might find Rufus, but the driver went straight to the Catholic church, which is about 300 metres from the school and *convento*.

The first thing Paul noticed was the number of Muslims surrounding the church. The Maranaos would normally stay away from churches, so it was a shock to see them walking in and out of the building. He recognised Rufus's friend Connie Balindong, a teacher in the school.

Connie came over to them, crying, 'I'm so sorry. Forgive me! Please, you Columbans, please forgive us here in Malabang for what we did to your priest.' She felt very ashamed that her friend had been killed by Maranaos. Her first cousin was the mayor and Rufus had often felt that nothing would happen to him because he was friends with the Balindongs.

Ben Maes met the three priests and said he would bring them to see Rufus's body before he presided over the Mass. He explained there would be no homily that day.

Paul felt a surge of anger at the sight of the press photographers in the church. He hadn't had a chance to see Rufus's remains yet, but from the door he could see them photographing the body lying in the glass coffin. He felt they should leave Rufus in peace.

Juan Cilliado came and hugged Paul, briefly telling him what had happened since Rufus's body was discovered. He cried when describing it. 'It must have been terrifying for him.'

'I know, Juan,' Paul replied.

He knew he couldn't put it off any longer, so he made his way into the church to see Rufus. When he saw him lying in the coffin, wearing a white soutane with a bandage around his head, Paul's sense of numbness and shock was instantly replaced by anguish and grief. He couldn't deny it; no mistake had been made. His friend lay dead in the coffin. It became all too real, and Paul broke down and cried for the first time since he had heard the news.

Colm stood by his side, noticing the details of how Rufus had been laid out by the embalmer. He had a set of brown rosary beads entwined through his right hand, while his left was partially covered. He wore a special stole with a Maranao design on it, and Colm thought he looked peaceful, although it was clear to him that he had met with a violent death.[1]

The local Maranao people started queuing up to sympathise with Paul and the other Columbans. Paul knew a lot of the people from the time he lived in Malabang.

The prison warden said, 'I'm so sorry for what they did to Fr Popong. He was my good friend, but don't worry, Father, when they catch the perpetrators of this crime I'll personally shoot them dead with my own gun,' and he brandished his gun.

Paul said nothing while he contemplated his answer. He could see the cultures clashing. It is common in Maranao culture to respond to violence with violence. He said in a measured tone, 'Personally, we priests would not like them to be shot dead.'

'Why? They killed your priest and he was a good man and he was my friend. If they are apprehended I will personally shoot them dead with my gun.'

Paul chose not to continue with the discussion, but he realised that his way of coping with death was very different. He also knew the last thing Rufus would want was for someone to be shot dead in retaliation for his death, and this thought stayed with him.[2]

***

As Yrap stood beside Rufus's body, he realised that he needed to talk to Celia to make sure she had heard the news. He tried to call her in Manila, but she was in another province in Batangas on a retreat as part of the Little Sisters' celebrations of their twenty-five years in the Philippines.

She returned to her house in Manila that evening and was in the middle of supper when Fr Chito rang. He spoke in a low voice because he was also on a retreat and was not supposed to be in touch with the outside world.

'Did you already hear about Popong?' he whispered.

'What happened?' Celia asked, not daring to speculate.

'Popong was ambushed.'

'Ambushed! He died?' she said in a hoarse voice.

'Yes, he died. I'm sorry,' he said.

After Chito's call, Celia went into a state of shock and wanted to go to Malabang straight away, but she remained where she was because she had to continue with the preparations for the celebration. It was only after her supervisor said she could attend his funeral that she departed.

***

After Mass, the Columbans and parishioners of Malabang met in the parish hall directly behind the church to decide where to bury the body. The tradition among the Columbans is that you are buried in the parish you die in. Rufus's will was kept in the Columban headquarters in Donaghmede in Dublin and they wanted to refer to it in case he had any particular requests in this regard. When they accessed it, it simply said in relation to his funeral, 'Bury me in the handiest spot you can find!'

Colm McKeating addressed the crowd of about eighty people, speaking in Tagalog, with Paul translating for him. He spoke about how Rufus had three families – the Columbans, his community in Malabang – Muslims and Christians who had become like family to him – and his natural family. He said it would be very risky for his Irish relatives to come to Malabang. He proposed that Rufus be buried in the Columban Fathers' plot in Cagayan de Oro, so that his Irish family could attend his funeral and access his final resting place. He proposed a period of mourning in Malabang, with the burial to take place in Cagayan de Oro on Saturday 1 September at 9 a.m. to allow sufficient time for people to travel back to Malabang before dark.

When most of the crowd said they wanted him buried in Malabang, Connie stood up and spoke: 'By holding the funeral in Malabang, emotions could run very high and add to tensions between the two communities. The funeral of a slain priest in a town with a strong military presence might exacerbate matters.'[3]

Her speech and passion changed the mood and when the crowd took a vote they decided he should be buried outside Malabang, with Cagayan de Oro chosen as the most suitable location.

So that Rufus's body would be available freely for Muslims to mourn him (because not all Muslims were ready to enter a church), it was decided to bring him to Our Lady of Peace High School.

The Columbans arranged Mass for Rufus for 9 a.m. the next day, Thursday 30 August, with Fr Nilo Tabania as the main celebrant. That evening Colm McKeating and Paul Glynn stayed in the *convento* where Rufus had lived. Colm noticed how simply Rufus lived; he had no fridge or air-conditioning. When Colm went to Rufus's room to gather some of his belongings, he found the heat unbearable and he very quickly became wet with sweat due to the lack of air and ventilation in the room. There was only one fan in the building, and it was in the living room.

When he woke the next morning, Colm went to the veranda overlooking the playground and saw white and black cloths pinned to the second floor of the school; Muslim and Christian signs of mourning. The flag was flying at half-mast. He saw Connie with the children gathering in the yard for assembly and went downstairs to her.

Connie invited him to speak to the staff and students, who were gathered in the bright morning sun. He called for peace and said there was a need to forgive each other and to create mutual acceptance. They needed to avoid recrimination.[4]

Afterwards, Connie pulled him aside and said that one of the six gunmen was in police custody. She said he told police that Abu Sayyaf had infiltrated Malabang and were attempting to recruit new members by offering an advance payment of 30,000–40,000 pesos to anyone who would join them. If anyone wanted to join them, however, they had to kidnap a foreigner to prove their allegiance. It was likely Rufus was a candidate for one such attempted kidnapping.[5]

That day the local papers carried a story that President Macapagal Arroyo denounced Rufus's murder and urged the police and military to intensify their efforts to catch the killers. The report said she was very concerned as to why the killings were still happening.[6]

Mass was scheduled for later that morning and Paul was asked to read the gospel at it. He noticed that many Muslims had entered the church. He started reading the gospel, trying to stay focused and not allow his grief to interfere with his delivery, when suddenly the door of the church burst open and Bebé ran in screaming, running straight to the coffin. She took off her shoe and started hitting the ground beside the coffin with it.

'Rufus, why didn't you listen to me? Why didn't you listen, you hard-headed fool? It's all dialogue, dialogue, dialogue,' she shouted between her gasping sobs. 'I told you. I warned you!'

She had constantly warned Rufus and Paul to be careful of kidnappers. Her family was subject to kidnap threats occasionally because it was well-off, so she knew what it was like to live in danger. She had been away visiting her son when Rufus died.

Paul stopped reading and paused for a few minutes to allow her time to calm herself. She didn't stop, though, so he eventually started the gospel again. Someone then politely took her into the room where she normally served the priests their meals, but the congregation could still hear her roaring. Yrap cried quietly throughout the Mass. Apart from the incident with Bebé, the Mass passed Paul by in a blur.

They transferred Rufus's body to the school in a procession that moved across the town plaza. Paul noticed a little Muslim boy shading the coffin with an ornate umbrella, the type usually reserved for a sultan's funeral.

At the school, they carried his body to the stage in the gymnasium, which was surrounded by flowers and decorated in a Maranao motif with Arabic greetings. They had written in English and Visayan: 'We love you Fr Popong. *Kini siya namatay aron mabuhi ug mamungag daghan.* [He died in order to live and bear much fruit.]'

Muslim students from the school chanted the Qur'an as he was carried in. It is a tradition among the Maranaos to recite the Qur'an during a wake to speed the person's journey back to God.

Priests, teachers and leaders of the community gathered on the stage, and the mayor of Malabang, Anwar Balindong, addressed the crowd. He offered his condolences on Rufus's death in English and spoke about his murder. He echoed what Connie had told Colm earlier that morning: Abu Sayyaf were offering people money to become members, and kidnapping foreigners was part of the initiation process. He pledged support to track down the killers and said he would resist all attempts by the extremist group to infiltrate Malabang.

They kept a vigil all night with speeches, prayers, testimonies and shared stories. People stayed in the school grounds, and many journalists stood around talking to the mourners. Mass on Friday was arranged for 6 a.m., but Colm got word that Bishop Edwin de la Peña, who had been at a conference in Bangkok at the time of Rufus's death, would return to preside over the Mass, but he would not arrive until 7.30 a.m. At the Mass, de la Peña read out a letter he had recently received from Rufus, saying that things were relatively quiet in Malabang, despite fears and warnings of kidnappings.

An old woman wearing a ragged dress ran out of the crowd and put flowers at the coffin saying, 'He was exceptional. You don't meet men like this every day.' Yrap recognised her as someone who had been good friends with Rufus; she was from one of the poorest families in the parish.

Afterwards, a convoy of thirty-seven vehicles was assembled to travel to the Immaculate Conception church in Bulua in Cagayan de Oro, where the funeral Mass would take place. As they left Malabang, with Rufus in the first car, people spontaneously created a guard of honour. Muslims and Christians lined the streets together, side by side, weeping for their friend. They were no longer two communities, but one community of people grieving together for someone they loved. The seed planted over many years of Muslim–Christian dialogue, now watered by his blood, had borne much fruit. In his death, as in his life, Rufus united people.

Paul sat in the second vehicle with Frs Nilo Tabania, Ben Maes and Colm McKeating. They all started crying at that point and cried for about an hour. Ben was driving and Colm had to say, 'Ben, watch the road so you don't crash.'

Muslims use white as a colour of mourning, so all the vehicles carried white flags. Along the way a little Maranao boy of about five put his hand up to greet the procession and said, 'Priest, have a safe journey.'

On the way to Cagayan de Oro, they stopped for about ten minutes in a predominately Christian area. They had all their windows open and the car was quiet. Whilst sitting there, Paul and his friends heard two Visayan girls talking. One said to the other, 'What are all these white flags about? There must be a wedding.'

Nilo turned around and said, 'Will there ever be any under-standing between the two communities if they are missing basic details like this?' Paul just shrugged; he had no answer.

That evening in Bulua a different atmosphere developed. People shared stories about Rufus, and Paul felt that it was like a reunion of friends. The relaxed mood was epitomised by Muslims and Christians sleeping in the church together.

For those who hadn't been to Malabang, however, it wasn't relaxed. Most of the Columbans hadn't seen Rufus yet and were stunned and appalled when they saw him and cried bitterly upon seeing his bandaged corpse.

Fr John Brannigan, who had arrived in the Philippines in 1969, the same year as Rufus, flew from Manila on Friday to attend his funeral. As he waited on the plane, a young woman approached him to check the flight details. In Tagalog she asked him, 'Are you a priest? Are you going to the funeral?'

She told him her name was Beibing and that she came from a poor family. She was bright, but her family had no money for education. Rufus had helped to finance her education from high school through to college. A few years previously she had been caught in an ambush near Balabagan, during which her father and brother were killed. She was left with serious leg injuries. Once again, Rufus had come to her aid and helped her pay for her hospital and rehabilitation costs.

She was attending Rufus's funeral against the wishes of her boss, who didn't want to give her time off. The journey had involved travelling six hours by road from her home in Pangasinan, in the north of the Philippines.

Fr John realised that although the trip probably cost her a month's salary, she willingly paid it so she could say goodbye to her friend.[7]

The Halley brothers – Gerry, Emmet, Eamonn, John and Walter – together with Donie Hogan, now assigned in Ireland, arrived in the Philippines the day before the funeral, while their mother remained with their sister in Canada. They arrived to a media circus at Manila International Airport, where a group of photographers and journalists mobbed the brothers as they walked through the bustling airport. They bombarded them with questions about their reaction to Rufus's murder, and couldn't believe it when the Halley brothers said they didn't want revenge. The Halley family stressed that their brother was a man of peace and his death should not be used as a reason for violence.

They overnighted in the Columban House in Singalong Street, flying to Cagayan de Oro on the morning of the funeral Mass. On landing, they went straight to the Columban house, where they met with more of Rufus's colleagues.

It appeared to Paul that they were still in shock, and their brother's death hadn't really hit them yet; they seemed outwardly calm, at first glance, although he could tell they were struggling to contain their emotions. They bore a striking physical resemblance to Rufus, with all five wearing the same straw hats.

The funeral Mass contained many of Rufus's favourite prayers and songs. Connie Balindong spoke about him at the Mass:

> We have lost a man of peace, a man of love, a man of understanding, but his vision will continue and his legacy will never die. Popong has become one of us. As a foreigner he even spoke Maranao more fluently than other Maranaos. Popong shared our problems as a member of the community.[8]

She went on to say that the Muslims had a special name for him – Alongan, which means 'Sun', because he radiated a light to those who came in contact with him.

Noriah Elias cried inconsolably on Paul's shoulders, asking him, 'Why is it that they always kill the good people and leave the bad to roam the streets?' Paul had the same question, so he couldn't answer; he simply cried alongside her.

Rufus's remains were carried out of the church to the sound

of one of his favourite songs, 'Time to Say Goodbye', sung by Andrea Bocelli and Sarah Brightman. It was a solemn and serene ceremony for a kind man.

Fr Rufus 'Popong' Halley was buried in Cagayan de Oro, under a jackfruit tree.

***

Although Rufus's friends and family members were scattered around the world at the time of his death, they were all impacted by the same grief when they heard the news. Venus was still in Ireland and on the day he was killed, she was visiting Fr John Meaney in St James's Hospital in Dublin. She was chatting with him when a man came over and said, 'Father, I've just heard the news that a Columban has been killed in the Philippines.'

'Oh my God,' the priest gasped, while Venus felt as if the wind had been knocked out of her.

'It must be Mindanao,' she said to him.

'I think that's the place,' he replied.

She started wondering who it might be, desperately trying to rule Rufus out of the equation. 'You would rule out Cagayan de Oro because no priests get killed there,' she said to Meaney, speaking quickly. 'That narrows the choices to Karomatan, Balabagan and Marawi.'

She went into denial and refused to speculate as to who it might be, because if she thought of anyone she would have thought of Popong. She refused to ask and soon said goodbye to Meaney, travelling back to Tullamore on the 4 p.m. train with an icy fear in her heart. She started chatting to the man opposite her, saying, 'I'm so worried. I'm really so worried about my friend.'

She arrived in Tullamore about 5 p.m. and went straight to the Blessed Sacrament Sisters to deliver a message.

Sister Teresa answered the door and before Venus could say anything, she asked, 'Did you know the priest who was killed?'

'Believe it or not, I don't,' Venus said, in her panicked state. Then she asked, 'Do you?', absolutely terrified of the answer.

Sister Teresa led her into the hall and said, 'It's a certain – gosh, it's an unusual name. Is there a Ru–?'

'Rufus Halley,' Venus finished for her, and then broke down. She was like a plant that wilted and she held onto the nun because the strength had gone from her legs.

'Oh God, I'm sorry. Did you know him?'

'Yes, I just didn't know it was him. He was here. He was in Tullamore in June,' Venus managed to say as they led her to a chair. She was in complete shock and the sisters asked her to stay the night with them, but she wanted to have her own space, so she returned to her rented house.

As soon as she got back, she rang Celia and they cried on the phone together. Venus felt so alienated, being on her own so far away from all her friends. 'Popong was so special,' she sobbed to her friend.

She rang Des in Dalgan Park, and he told her there would be services for Rufus there and in his hometown of Waterford. She knew she couldn't return to the Philippines for the funeral, so she had to mourn her friend in his home country.

Feeling a strong need to ritualise his loss, she made an altar in her bedroom. Throughout the night, she lit candles and kept vigil, praying for him and looking at his photo, waking him in her own way.

CHAPTER 21

Men are so accustomed to maintaining external order by violence
that they cannot conceive of life being possible without violence.

Leo Tolstoy

The story of the missionary's death made headlines around the world. Newspapers in Ireland and the Philippines dedicated dozens of pages to it over several days, and they offered different thoughts on who may have been responsible.

The eyes of the world were on the Filipino police force and they were using all their resources to identify the suspects, of which there were six.[1] By Thursday 30 August, Superintendent Omar Ali said they had arrested two suspects: the alleged lookout during the botched kidnapping, Canal Macapodi, and twenty-five-year-old Abdulsamad Ibrahim (also referred to as Ibrahim Samad), who allegedly told police he had driven the Second World War military truck containing the six armed men. He also allegedly told the police chief they planned to turn Rufus over to the Abu Sayyaf extremist rebels, and that Atto Sumagayan Daing, the eldest son of former MNLF commander Datu Daing, was the leader of their armed gang.

The suspects were reported to have taken refuge at the MILF's Camp Jubal Nul. The MILF denied that the suspected killers belonged to their group, and police could not enter the camp to search for them because that would have violated the ceasefire that was in place between the MILF and the government.

While the police rounded up the suspects in the Philippines, the Halley brothers arrived back in Ireland, where they held a Mass for Rufus in his home parish of Butlerstown in Waterford.

Hundreds of people turned out to pay their respects to the man they had loved. He was well known in the parish as he often said Mass when he returned home on holidays. The Irish congregation always loved when he said Mass – he was so ordinary and could still identify with the people, despite living outside Ireland for most of his life.

Des Hartford and Bishop William Lee concelebrated, while Donie Hogan gave the homily. It was very emotional and Des broke down during the Mass. He was unable to contain the swell of emotions and grief he felt for his friend. The church was so packed with people who wanted to say their last goodbyes that loudspeakers played outside for those who stood in the dreary weather.

Rufus's mother, Imelda, and sister, Evelyn, travelled from Canada for the Mass and the Halley family sat together, trying to come to terms with their loss. Gerry quietly tried to accept his own sadness during the ceremony, which celebrated the life of the man they'd all adored. They all knew Rufus was different; every time he came home all the family hoped he would stay with them. He was always full of ideas and exciting stories. Gerry knew they were lucky to have had him in their lives. He had been a marvellous example of what the church could be.

Two days later, on 11 September 2001, the Columbans held a memorial Mass for Rufus in Dalgan Park, where he'd trained. Kevin McHugh was back in Ireland at this time and he organised the liturgy. Venus assisted him. At one point, he asked her to photocopy some sheets for the Mass, and when she went into the room to use the photocopier she saw several priests engrossed in the television. She didn't have time to stop but wondered why people would watch TV during the preparations for Rufus's Mass. It was only later in the day that she learned about the terrorist attacks in America. This reinforced to her how important the work of dialogue was between conflicting communities.

Kevin McHugh was the main celebrant during the Mass. Des was the homilist and he noticed how numb everyone appeared to be. Dave Cribbin and Kevin looked drained, and Venus wept quietly throughout. Des reflected on the last conversation he had with his friend and how Rufus had been so sure that the goodness of people would win out in the end. *It was Rufus's goodness that won out*, Des thought. He really did end up like Charles de Foucauld in the end, he pondered, thinking about how the French missionary died at the hands of Muslim bandits, although he had spent so many years living his faith alongside them in their community.

***

Rufus's murder changed everything in the prelature. In the aftermath, there was a lot of suspicion that these kidnappings were not the work of religious fanatics. Some suspected that Rufus's death was the work of drug addicts. When Paul Glynn went back for Rufus's forty days 'month's mind' in Malabang, he heard rumours that a prominent local gangster might have masterminded the attempted kidnapping, so he could sell Rufus to other gangs.[2] Paul was very frightened going home from the month's mind Mass. His friends had told him to be extra careful because the suspected kidnapper was living in the area, so he travelled by boat. Other rumours attributed the murder to 'The Pentagon Group', a terrorist group that broke away from the MILF earlier that year to continue kidnapping. A climate of fear perpetuated these rumours.

About six weeks after Rufus's death, an Italian priest called Pier Antoni was kidnapped near Pagadian. He was held for five months and twenty-two days. This confirmed that Rufus's attempted kidnapping was not a one-off.

Paul decided that he wouldn't let fear rule his life and continued doing his work as normal. About two weeks later he went to the Columban house in Manila for a meeting. When he came back, Mieta, the secretary, told him that she had received a phone call from an anonymous caller, who had asked, 'Is this the Columban Fathers?' When the reply was in the affirmative, the voice said, 'The Americano priest who knows how to speak "minuslim" had better watch out because he might be kidnapped.'

All white foreigners were referred to as 'Americanos' because of the American influence in the Philippines. The fact that the caller was looking for someone who spoke the Muslim language suggested that it was a Christian speaking, as there is no such thing as a Muslim or 'minuslim' language. The Muslims in the Philippines speak different languages depending on where they live, just like the Christians.

The phone call had the desired effect, and Paul became very frightened. He decided not to return to the *barrio* where he was living; he went to the Columban house in Ozamiz instead, where he stayed for about a week.

Bishop Edwin de la Peña called all the Marawi-based priests to a meeting at the Mercy Hospital in Iligan. They had a long discussion about whether Paul should go back to Sigayan or not and whether Ben Maes should stay where he was in Balabagan. There was some evidence that people were trying to kidnap him and one of the Franciscan priests had also heard rumours that military people were involved in the kidnappings.

'Paul, we can't take any chances. The suspicions are very strong that the military were involved in the kidnappings, and they can use any means at their disposal. If they want to get to you, they'll get you. You and Ben should leave Marawi,' de la Peña said.

They agreed they had to leave for their own safety. Paul moved to Ozamiz, where he stayed for three months.

'It was so bad that I didn't even go back to collect my things. Fred, the man who drove the jeep to me to tell me Rufus had died that night, picked up my belongings,' he remembers.

He felt as if he were in exile because he couldn't go back to his house. People from the village came to visit him in Ozamiz. He never found out who made the phone call, but because they used the word 'minuslim' he knew they didn't know anything about the Muslim languages and surmised it may have been a military person trying to warn him.

While Paul was in exile in Ozamiz, his colleague Gerry Sheehy also received threatening messages from would-be kidnappers. He got the same message about the Americano who knew how to speak 'minuslim' being kidnapped. He phoned the house in Ozamiz to relay the information and said, 'I feel they must be talking about Paul Glynn', as only a small number of white priests spoke Maranao and worked in Marawi.

This made the decision for Paul. His superior, Fr Neil Collins, suggested that he go home and take a good break. He returned to Ireland in February 2002 and started studying for a Masters at the School of Economics in London in September, only returning to the Philippines in May 2004.

Following Rufus's death, Yrap went to Balabagan for a week and observed the people in that community grieving too. After the burial, the clergy met in Cagayan de Oro. Yrap said he couldn't go back to the house in Malabang, so he transferred to Balabagan. Yrap tried to continue Rufus's legacy by organising trips to the prison with food and other gifts. He organised a group of Christian volunteers to help manage the visits to ensure the prisoners received regular visits.

After some time, Yrap discovered that Abdulsamad Ibrahim, one of the men accused of murdering Rufus, was in prison. They had a discussion about whether they should visit him and treat him like any other prisoner. Although Yrap felt burdened with grief and pain, and part of him didn't want to authorise the visit, he knew that he wouldn't be following Rufus's legacy if he said no. The group made sure to visit the accused man. This was a hard visit for them, but they had learned that the road to peace was long and painful.

Afterwards, when some people said that Rufus was careless with his life, it annoyed Yrap because he knew the truth. Rufus was far from careless – he had simply known the best way to handle things. He felt it would be better to show his courage and his contempt for the greed of these people. Although he loved life, he lost his while trying to help stop the cycle of kidnappings and violence.

CHAPTER 22

As we are liberated from our own fear, our
presence automatically liberates others.

Nelson Mandela

Des felt ready to return to the Philippines by the autumn of
2001. He wasn't sure where he would live, but he was clear that
he wouldn't go back to Marawi – Bishop de la Peña had taken
over his role as apostolic administrator of the prelature of St
Mary's and Des didn't want him to feel that he was looking over
his shoulder.

He didn't feel relaxed enough to go to Marawi on a visit, so
he spent time in the various Columban houses in Cagayan de
Oro and Ozamiz, talking to his superiors about his next move.
He wanted to do the retreat work but also wanted to remain
involved pastorally with people.

He ended up in a small parish in Ozamiz, which gave him
time to run retreats while also taking care of his parishioners'
needs. He was getting quite a number of demands for retreat
work and was very settled and happy.

Venus Guibone returned to the Philippines in April 2002
and started working with Des. They did weeks of guided
prayer, where members of the community would do five or six-
day retreats, during which time they would meet with Venus,
Des and others as their retreat guides, chatting about their
experiences.

'This is my dream, Venus,' Des said to her one day. 'I just want
something ordinary. I would love to continue to do this.'

Venus worked with him throughout the summer and was

then invited back to Ireland. She didn't know what to do, so she decided to talk to Des about it.

'Des, I've been invited back to a parish in Ireland. I know I'm involved with the retreats here, and I really want to continue to support you. Saying that, I feel drawn back to Ireland. Just for a year or two,' she said. 'I don't understand why I'm feeling this way, Des, and maybe that's why sometimes I'm not at peace – a lot of things go on. And there are a lot of things in my mind.'

'Venus, just own the decision to go back and be at peace. Think nothing else,' he replied.

Venus immediately felt reassured. 'Oh, Des, I'd love to continue helping you with these retreats. I'll only be there for two years. I have no intention of staying in Ireland.'

'Stop worrying; you must do what you feel drawn to. God blesses the desires of your heart.'

Venus returned to Ireland and Des continued in his pastoral work.

***

The Catholics, Protestants and Muslims had started having interfaith meetings in Pagadian, which had been set up specifically to discuss issues that were important to the people on the ground: drug issues, criminality, poverty and other problems that directly affected the ordinary people.

Sultan Maguid Maruhom had been a member of the group for a year when Des came along to a meeting. Maguid was happy to see him but wondered why he was there.[1]

'Why did you come back to the Philippines after you lost your position in Marawi?' Maguid asked with typical directness.

Des didn't immediately answer. He didn't explain that he hadn't in fact lost his position and that he was happy to hand it back to a Filipino bishop. He looked into the distance for a few moments, gathering his thoughts. 'Anyway I'm here. Do you think it's right for me to come back?'

'No, I personally don't think so, because you don't have your position.'

'What about Pagadian? Is it okay for me to be here?'

'No, personally I don't think you're safe here.'

Another priest, Fr Pier Antoni, had recently been kidnapped and Maguid wasn't sure who would be next.

'Would it be okay if I come here to visit?' Des enquired.

'Yes, that would probably be fine.'

'Can I stay in Ozamiz? Is it safe?'

'Yes, it's safe. There are foreigners there,' Maguid replied evenly, though he wondered what Des could really do in Ozamiz.

Their friendship had a long-lasting effect on Maguid. The sultan found it difficult to be vulnerable around people and saw how it seemed to come more easily to Des. Because of his background, growing up in a violent society, Maguid had a clear understanding of what justice looked like, but love, in particular spiritual love, was something he struggled with. He spoke to Des about it sometimes, who advised him that strength comes from love and forgiveness.

'You have to learn to forgive. You have to exercise the forgiveness.'

'I am a sultan. I am supposed to be able to protect my people and to survive. I should be strong.'

'Sometimes we don't understand that how we act is brave. Bravery has a tender side and can come from love. You need to replace the anger with love, so you can live in peace,' Des advised.

With those few words, he changed the sultan's life. Maguid learned not to be afraid anymore. Although he was still in danger, he stopped carrying a gun. He started serving people again and teaching them how to live in peace. He thought it was important for people to know justice, but he now believed that justice could not exist without love. He had seen Des living this way with Muslims.

Maguid had often felt worthless – that he wasn't useful to society – but the love Des radiated towards everyone was clear to him, and he felt Des's genuine warmth. He thought that many Muslims in his region lacked this warmth because of their lived experience. He started studying the Qur'an every day, until he gained a deeper knowledge of it. He discovered why Islam in Mindanao was so full of retribution and revenge.

'We were taught how to hate people. Some ulama taught hatred and anger in their prayers,' he said.

He had previously allowed others to interpret the Qur'an for him, but now he started to analyse it himself.

Because the Qur'an is written in Arabic, it is open to the interpretation of each translator. Maguid asked some local imams to translate the original text and he learned that there is no pronoun in front of the word anger (or wrath). It just says those who earned anger.

'The opening prayer in the Qur'an says, "Lead us on the straight path. The path of those to whom you have bestowed your Grace, not those who earned anger because they went astray." They repeat it four times in prayer,' Maguid said. 'This prayer is used by fundamentalists to explain why they hate people who are not Muslims. Some Muslims interpret this line to hate those who don't follow Islam.'

When he read the Qur'an, he never read anywhere that Allah is angry. Only that He is merciful. This led him to question what he had been taught over the years.

'How can you be in *jihad* if you have no anger? How can you kill people if you don't believe Allah is angry with people? I had lived for years in the dark, in fear and frustration, but I suddenly felt light fall upon me,' he said.

He espoused this new message of love and forgiveness to everyone he met, and it gradually started having an effect on those closest to him. He decided to forgive Naga Dimaporo's son, Motalib, who had allegedly killed his brother.

His nephew couldn't get over the murder and was sick with anger and frustration, but Maguid kept trying to lead him to the path of forgiveness and peace, rather than the way of retribution. Some time later his nephew was attending Mecca, when he saw Motalib on the other side of the street. Both men crossed into the middle of the street and embraced.

Motalib said, 'Forgive me.'

Maguid's nephew replied with the same words. It was an impulsive gesture on his part, but it seemed to put an end to the *rido* and rivalry between the families. When Maguid made forgiveness his policy, the killing stopped. Although the rivalry has never been publicly or formally finished, things have quietened down. He knew that if he hadn't met Des, this might not have happened. Some people in the region say *rido* is part of their culture, but the sultan doesn't believe that now.

'The Filipinos were a peaceful people – they gave land to Muslims and Christians. The land for the church came from my father. It came from love because my father was not educated. He acted according to his values.'

Love was practised by Des in his own way, too, living with Muslims. Because of this, Maguid made it his mission to promote justice and love.

'There is no hope for this world without this,' he said.

***

Fr Des was enjoying a peaceful time in his life, facilitating retreats, when one day he noticed he had a cyst on his head.

The doctor told him not to worry, but prescribed antibiotics and referred him to a dermatologist, who sent him to Manila for tests. It was there, in September 2002, that the cyst was diagnosed as high-grade malignant. He had skin cancer. A week later he was on a plane back to Ireland, where the doctors removed the cyst and started him on a course of chemotherapy.

Des moved into the Columban Fathers' House in Dalgan Park in Navan and received his treatment in the Mater Hospital in Dublin. However, his cancer got progressively more aggressive and spread, despite radiation and chemotherapy. Des grew weaker. He had seen enough deaths to know that he wasn't going to recover.

In a letter to Kevin McHugh in February 2004, he acknowledged his imminent death. 'My situation is serious. … [the specialist] has given me all the major treatments available and they have not worked. Any further heavy treatment could be detrimental to my quality of life, rather than enhance it.'[2]

He went on to say that he had faith where he would go when he died. He wasn't afraid to die, or to meet God, though he was afraid of a painful death.

Venus visited him often and they spent hours chatting about their faith. One time she facilitated a mini-retreat near Dalgan Park with a group of women from Tullamore. She asked Des to say Mass and he made a deep impact on them.

When she arrived for a visit on 12 March 2004, she discovered he had become very weak and had slipped into a coma. Fr Pat Raleigh told her to go into Des's bedroom, where his brother and sister were with him.

The four of them stayed with him throughout the night. They could see he was slipping away. Every two hours a different

Columban came into the room and prayed with them. The following morning several people gathered around Des's bed and Pat led the rosary.

After Des had received his diagnosis, he wrote a poem called 'Briared Daffodil', which was about living with cancer. When they finished praying, Pat handed a framed copy of it to Venus, saying, 'Venus, would you mind reading this?'

Everyone in the room was aware that Des was slipping away quietly. With each breath, his breathing grew shallower. Venus picked up the frame and started reading his poem as if it were a prayer. Most people in the room held hands. Her voice was sure but gentle as she read:

> Amidst brooding winter darkness,
> Cancer and chemotherapy
> Bring fears of pain, loneliness and death.
>
> Future plans discarded,
> Life is offered on God's terms, not mine.
> Depend on His Love.
>
> Suffering acknowledged
> Crowned Christ is in the pain
> Hope in His desire to heal.

Venus paused for a moment and looked at the man lying in front of her. She had her hand on his knee, and someone was holding her shoulders. She glanced at the time and noticed it was 9.35 a.m. She could still hear his gentle breathing. She gave her attention to the poem once again and continued with the last stanza:

Suffering transformed,
The Risen Saviour lives within,
Like a briared daffodil bursting forth …

With those words Des gave his final breath and the people in the room could almost feel him being released from his sick body.

My God; what have you made me experience? Venus thought to herself. With tears rolling down her face, she read the last line of the poem like a mantra:

Believe and be at peace!
Believe and be at peace, Des.
Believe and be at peace.

Fr Des Hartford died peacefully, surrounded by his friends and family members, on 13 March 2004.

EPILOGUE

No one was ever charged with the murder of Lydia Macas. No one was ever charged with the abduction of Fr Des Hartford. No one was found guilty of Fr Rufus Halley's death. Abdulsamad Ibrahim's case went to trial in 2003, but he was acquitted.

The island of Mindanao continues to be a place where violent deaths frequently occur. Since Rufus Halley was killed, there have been many terrorist attacks and kidnappings targeting not just foreign missionaries but also tourists.

In 2017, the 'Battle of Marawi' took place, when armed militants took hold of the city and got into combat with the army. Filipino priest Fr Teresito Suganob was captured during this event, along with fifteen of his parishioners, and kept hostage for almost four months. This prolonged 'battle' cost over 800 lives.

Alongside the atrocities, however, the dialogue of life and faith is alive and continues in the region. The labours of Des and Rufus for Muslim–Christian dialogue have borne fruit.

Venus Guibone, now working in St John Vianney Theological Seminary in Cagayan de Oro, is still involved in works for peace and reconciliation. After the Battle of Marawi in 2017, she engaged with Muslim and Christian volunteers in reaching out to displaced Maranaos. She helped organise solidarity visits to Piagapo in Lanao del Sur (about six kilometres from Marawi city), which hosted many displaced Maranaos. Their solidarity visits consisted of relief distribution; psychosocial processing for children, youths and adults; feeding and hygiene education.

This type of work with the displaced victims of conflict is inter-religious dialogue at its best. Christians and Muslims

(Maranaos) worked closely together and it brought everyone closer to the spirit of dialogue. Venus thought of Des and Rufus with every visit.

Other Irish missionaries, Filipino priests and lay people continue to work for peace and dialogue in the region.

Paul Glynn, who now lives and works in Manila as regional director of the Columbans, continues to support the Interfaith Forum in the Archdiocese of Cagayan de Oro in Mindanao.

Yrap Nazareno is based in Libona, Bukidnon, working as parish priest and living Bishop Tudtud's vision.

Despite the violence in the region, the friendships forged by Rufus and Des have had long-lasting effects. Many ordinary Muslims and Christians work together to create peace, alongside the ulama, priests and bishops.

ENDNOTES

INTRODUCTION

1 In April 1898, America declared war against Spain when it began a blockade of Cuba in support of Cuban independence from Spain. The conflict moved from Cuba to the Philippines when the United States took control of Spain's colonies, including Puerto Rico, Guam and the Philippines.

2 Collins, N., *The Splendid Cause: The Missionary Society of St Columban, 1916–1954* (Columba Press, Dublin, 2009), pp. 187–9.

3 *Ibid.*, p. 189.

4 Ó Murchú, P., *Mission in an Era of Change: The Columbans 1963–2014* (Red Hen Publishing, Kerry, 2014), p. 34.

5 The 1935 Constitution of the Philippines, accessed via *Official Gazette*: www.officialgazette.gov.ph/constitutions/the-1935-constitution. Accessed 12 January 2019.

6 Evolution of the Philippine Constitution, accessed via *Official Gazette*: www.officialgazette.gov.ph/constitutions/1935-constitution-ammended. Accessed 12 January 2019.

CHAPTER 1

1 Dolan, R. E., *Philippines: A Country Study* (Library of Congress, Washington, 1993), p. 52. Accessed 16 December 2010 from http://countrystudies.us/philippines/28.htm.

2 Ó Murchú (2014), p. 16.

3 Larousse, W., *A Local Church Living for Dialogue: Muslim-Christian Relations in Mindanao-Sulu, Philippines* (Gregorian University Press, Rome, 2001), p. 150.

4 *Ibid.*

5 Ó Murchú (2014), p. 17.

6 Collins (2009), p. 193.

7 *Ibid.*, p. 186.

8 *Ibid.*

9 *Ibid.*, p. 190.

10 In Catholicism, the Eucharist, or communion, is the term for the

bread and wine when transubstantiated (their substance changed) into the body and blood of Jesus Christ.

CHAPTER 2

1 Timberman, D. G., *A Changeless Land: Continuity and Change in Philippine Politics* (Routledge, London, 1991), p. 57.

2 Larousse (2001), p. 136.

3 George, T. J. S., *Revolt in Mindanao: The Rise of Islam in Philippine Politics* (Oxford University Press, Oxford, 1980), p. 164.

4 Larousse (2001), p. 467.

5 Tudtud, B., *Dialogue of Life and Faith: Selected Writings of Bishop Bienvenido Tudtud* (Claretian Publications, Quezon, 1988), p. 77.

6 Larousse (2001), p. 467.

7 The Catholic Bishops' Conference of the Philippines, 2004 – http://cbcpwebsite.com/ArchDioceses2/marawi.html. Accessed 18 November 2010.

8 Tudtud (1988), pp. 102–4.

9 *Ibid.*, p. 79.

10 *Ibid.*, pp. 146–50.

11 Author interview with Des Hartford, Dalgan Park, 20 January 2004.

12 *Ibid.*

CHAPTER 3

1 Tudtud (1988), p. 45.

2 *Barrio* is the Spanish word for neighbourhood and means 'rural village' in the Philippines.

CHAPTER 4

1 Author interview with Seán McDonagh, Dalgan Park, 21 June 2016.

2 Rufus means 'red-haired' in Latin.

3 The Columbans served a term of seven years at a time. Between each term, they had approximately six months off. Most of them went back to Ireland and took holidays between terms.

4 http://www.vatican.va/news_services/liturgy/saints/ns_lit_doc_20051113_de-foucauld_en.html. Accessed 20 October 2014.

5 *Ibid.*

6 Email from Louie Jalandoni to Fr Colm McKeating, 30 August 2001.

7 Larousse (2001), p. 158.

8 *Ibid.*, p. 162. 'Leader of the Moro Islamic Front Outlines His Vision for the Future from His Jungle Base.'

9 *Ibid.*, p. 161.

10 *Ibid.*

11 Author interview with Venus Guibone, Mindanao, 4 July 2005.

12 *Business World Online*, 16 November 2015: 'The truth about the economy under the Marcos regime': http://www.bworldonline. com/content.php?section=Opinion&title=the-truth-about-the-economy-under-the-marcosregime&id=118661. Accessed 9 June 2016.

CHAPTER 5

1 The Tablighs are Muslim missionaries who studied overseas, particularly in the Indian subcontinent. This was originally done in order to revive Islam in Pakistan. They concentrated on the spiritual aspect of Islam and were interested in the purity of Islamic doctrine.

CHAPTER 6

1 Letter from Rufus Halley to Celia Eco, Balabagan, Lanao del Sur, 15 November 1987.

2 Author interview with Sr Celia Eco, Cagayan de Oro, 9 July 2005.

CHAPTER 7

1 Author interview with Maguid Maruhom, Pagadian, 5 July 2005.

CHAPTER 8

1 Letter from Rufus Halley to Gerry Halley, London, date unknown.

2 Author interview with John Robinson by phone, 11 November 2009.

3 Letter from Rufus Halley to his father, Glasgow, no date.

4 *Ibid.*

5 Charismatics is a diverse form of Christianity that emphasises the Holy Spirit and expects that modern-day miracles will be part of a person's life.

6 Letter from Rufus Halley to Celia Eco, Tunisia, 23 October 1993.

CHAPTER 9

1 Letter from Rufus Halley to Celia Eco, Malabang, 20 November 1994.

2 An autonomous region that has the authority to control its culture and economy, created by Republic Act No. 6734.

3 Letter from Rufus Halley to John Robinson, Malabang, 18 January 1996.

4 Rufus was referencing a verse from John 12:24.

5 Letter from Rufus Halley to Celia Eco, Waterford, 1 April 1996.

6 Letter from Rufus Halley to Celia Eco, Malabang, 13 August 1996.

CHAPTER 10

1 A hostage is used in a negotiation. A kidnapping could be for a myriad of reasons, and many kidnappers never have any intention of releasing their victims. Hostages are usually released once the point of negotiation has been reached and resolved.

CHAPTER 11

1 The NPUDC was an organisation mandated to assist former rebels in getting jobs or setting up livelihood projects.

CHAPTER 12

1 *The Irish Times*, 3 November 1997.

2 *People's Tonight*, 7 November 1997.

3 The Organisation of Islamic Cooperation (OIC) is the collective voice of the Muslim world with a membership of fifty-seven states across the world.

CHAPTER 13

1 Letter from Donie Hogan to Joe Hayes, Manila, 2 November 1997.

CHAPTER 14

1 Dan O'Malley, post-kidnap interview with Des Hartford, Maynooth, December 1997.

CHAPTER 15

1   Dan O'Malley, post-kidnap interview with Des Hartford, May-nooth, December 1997.

2   https://www.ucanews.com/story-archive/?post_name=/1997/11/21/release-of-kidnapped-belgian-priest-leaves-unsettled-issues&post_id=10432. Accessed 17 November 2015.

3   Letter from Rufus Halley to Celia Eco, Malabang, December 1997.

4   Letter from Rufus Halley to Celia Eco, Malabang, February/March 1998.

5   Letter from Rufus Halley to Celia Eco, Malabang, August/September 1998.

6   *Ibid.*

CHAPTER 16

1   Halley, R., 'A Magic Moment in Marawi', *Misyon* (November/December 2000), pp. 12–13.

2   Letter from Rufus Halley to Celia Eco, Malabang, 1998 (month unknown).

3   Letter from Rufus Halley to Celia Eco, Daguyon, 13 February 1999.

CHAPTER 17

1   Letter from Rufus Halley to Celia Eco, Daguyon, 13 February 1999.

2   Letter from Rufus Halley to Celia Eco, Waterford, 1 July 1999.

3   Author interview with John Robinson by phone, 11 November 2009.

CHAPTER 18

1   *Pasalubong* is a Tagalog word that means to bring someone back a gift from your travels.

2   https://www.irishtimes.com/news/44-die-in-philippines-bus-bombs-1.249414. Accessed 20 November 2009.

3   http://news.bbc.co.uk/2/hi/asia-pacific/658002.stm. Accessed 20 November 2009.

4   https://www.newspapers.com/newspage/17709265/. Accessed 20 November 2009.

5 Joseph Estrada, a former actor, was president from 1998 to 2001, after which he was impeached for corruption. In 2007, he was sentenced to lifetime imprisonment for stealing $80 million from the government. Gloria Macapagal Arroyo, his former vice-president, then became president. In October 2007, just six weeks after his conviction, she granted him a pardon.

6 Alan's Point – History and Contemporary Events, 'AFP-MILF 2000 War in Mindanao Remembered': http://alan73.blogspot.com/2008/10/afp-milf-2000-war.html. Accessed 20 November 2009.

7 'Priest determined not to say Mass at Camp', *Philippines Today*, 18 August 2000.

8 *Ibid.*

9 Alan's Point – History and Contemporary Events: http://alan73.blogspot.com/2008/10/afp-milf-2000-war.html. Accessed 20 November 2009.

CHAPTER 19

1 Letter from Rufus Halley to Celia Eco, Malabang, 26 August 2000.

2 Letter from Rufus Halley to his brother Gerry, Malabang, 4 March 2001.

3 Letter from Rufus Halley to his sister Evelyn in Canada, Malabang, July 2001.

4 McKeating, C., 'Report on the Tragic Death of Rufus Halley' (unpublished report, Manila, 2001), p. 2.

CHAPTER 20

1 McKeating (2001), p. 3.

2 Author interview with Paul Glynn, Mindanao, 6 July 2005.

3 McKeating (2001), p. 3.

4 *Ibid.*, p. 5.

5 *Ibid.*

6 *The Philippine Daily Inquirer*, 29 August 2001, p. 15.

7 Brannigan, J., 'Death of a Peacemaker', *Far East* (November 2001), pp. 10–11.

8 'Muslims join Christians in mourning "Fr. Popong"', *The Philippine Star*, 2 September 2001, p. 4.

CHAPTER 21

1 'Second suspect in slaying of Irish priest arrested', *The Philippine Star*, 1 September 2001, p. 4.

2 A month's mind is a Mass celebrated about a month after a person dies; it is celebrated in their memory.

CHAPTER 22

1 Author interview with Maguid Maruhom, Pagadian, 5 July 2005.

2 Letter from Des to Kevin McHugh, Dalgan Park, 9 February 2004.

BIBLIOGRAPHY

Books

Collins, N., *The Splendid Cause: The Missionary Society of St Columban, 1916–1954* (Columba Press, Dublin, 2009)

Collins, N., *A Mad Thing to Do: A Century of Columban Missions* (Dalgan Press, Meath, 2017)

Decasa, G., *The Qur'anic Concept of Umma and Its Function in Philippine Muslim Society* (Gregorian Biblical Bookshop, Rome, 1999)

Dolan, R. E., *Philippines: A Country Study* (Library of Congress, Washington, 1993)

George, T. J. S., *Revolt in Mindanao: The Rise of Islam in Philippine Politics* (Oxford University Press, Oxford, 1980)

Larousse, W., *A Local Church Living for Dialogue: Muslim–Christian Relations in Mindanao–Sulu, Philippines* (Gregorian University Press, Rome, 2001)

McAmis, R. D., *Malay Muslims: The History and Challenge of Resurgent Islam in Southeast Asia* (William Eerdmans, Cambridge, 2002)

McCoy, A. W., *Priests on Trial: Father Gore and Father O'Brien Caught in the Crossfire between Dictatorship and Revolution* (Penguin, London, 1984)

O'Brien, N., *Seeds of Injustice. Reflections on the Murder Frame-up of the Negros Nine in the Philippines* (O'Brien Press, Dublin, 1985)

O'Brien, N., *Revolution from the Heart* (Veritas, Dublin, 1988)

Ó Murchú, P. , *Mission in an Era of Change: The Columbans 1963–2014* (Red Hen Publishing, Kerry, 2014)

Riedinger, J. M., *Agrarian Reform in the Philippines: Democratic Transitions and Redistributive Reform* (Stanford University Press, Redwood City, 1995)

Rodil, B., *The Minoritization of the Indigenous Communities of Mindanao and the Sulu Archipelago* (Alternate Forum for Research in Mindanao, Davao, 1994)

Timberman, D. G., *A Changeless Land: Continuity and Change in Philippine Politics* (Routledge, London, 1991)

Tudtud, B., *Dialogue of Life and Faith: Selected Writings of Bishop Bienvenido Tudtud* (Claretian Publications, Quezon, 1988)

Wright, C., *Charles de Foucauld: Journey of the Spirit* (Pauline Books and Media, Boston, 2005)

Correspondence

Capalla, F. to Colm McKeating and Richard Pankratz, Davao, 31 August 2001

Halley, R. to Evelyn Donnelly, Malabang, July 2001

Halley, R. to Sr Celia Eco, Balabagan, Lanao del Sur, 15 November 1987

Halley, R. to Sr Celia Eco, Tunisia, 23 October 1993

Halley, R. to Sr Celia Eco, Malabang, 20 November 1994

Halley, R. to Sr Celia Eco, Cotabato, 19 February 1995

Halley, R. to Sr Celia Eco, Malabang, 20 April 1995

Halley, R. to Sr Celia Eco, Malabang, 25 July 1995

Halley, R. to Sr Celia Eco, Malabang, 15 September 1995

Halley, R. to Sr Celia Eco, Waterford, 1 April 1996

Halley, R. to Sr Celia Eco, Malabang, 13 August 1996

Halley, R. to Sr Celia Eco, Malabang, 18 December 1996

Halley, R. to Sr Celia Eco, Malabang, 30 January 1997

Halley, R. to Sr Celia Eco, London, 24 April 1997

Halley, R. to Sr Celia Eco, Malabang, 20 October 1997

Halley, R. to Sr Celia Eco, Malabang, December 1997

Halley, R. to Sr Celia Eco, Malabang, February/March 1998

Halley, R. to Sr Celia Eco, Malabang, August/September 1998

Halley, R. to Sr Celia Eco, Malabang, 1998

Halley, R. to Sr Celia Eco, Daguyon, 13 February 1999

Halley, R. to Sr Celia Eco, Waterford, 1 July 1999

Halley, R. to Sr Celia Eco, September/October 1999

Halley, R. to Sr Celia Eco, Malabang, 27 May 2000

Halley, R. to Sr Celia Eco, Malabang, 26 August 2000

Halley, R. to Sr Celia Eco, Malabang, 2 September 2000

Halley, R. to Sr Celia Eco, Balabagan, 10 January 2001

Halley, R. to his father, Glasgow, no date

Halley, R. to Deb and Gerry Halley, Malabang, 4 March 2001

Halley, R. to Gerry Halley, London, 1990

Halley, R. to Gerry Halley, London, no date

Halley, R. to John Robinson, Malabang, 18 January 1996

Halley, R. to John Robinson, Malabang, 10 February 1997

Hartford, D. to Kevin McHugh, Dalgan Park, 9 February 2004

Hogan, D. to Irish Ambassador Joe Hayes, Manila, 2 November 1997

Jalandoni, L. to Fr Colm McKeating, via email, 30 August 2001

Interviews

Ballindong, C., Marawi State University, Philippines, 8 July 2005

Bernaldez, E., Mindanao, Philippines, 5 July 2005

Eco, C., Cagayan de Oro, Mindanao, Philippines, 9 July 2005

Elias, N., Marawi State University, Philippines, 8 July 2005

Glynn, P., Cagayan de Oro, Mindanao, Philippines, 4–6 July 2005

Guibone, V., Cagayan de Oro, Mindanao, Philippines, 4 July 2005

Guibone, V., Dalgan Park, Navan, Ireland, 8 February 2017

Halley, G., Waterford, Ireland, 26 January 2005

Hartford, D., Maynooth, Ireland, December 1997 (post-kidnap interview done by D. O'Malley)

Hartford, D., Dalgan Park, Navan, Ireland, 16 January 2004

Hartford, D., Dalgan Park, Navan, Ireland, 20 January 2004

Hartford, D., Dalgan Park, Navan, Ireland, 23 January 2004

Hartford, D., Dalgan Park, Navan, Ireland, 27 January 2004

Hogan, D., Ballymun, Dublin, Ireland, dates during 2004

Hogan, D., Dalgan Park, Navan, Ireland, dates during 2016, 2017, 2018 and 2019

Hurley, B., phone interview, 11 November 2009

Macarandas, E., Marawi State University, Philippines, 8 July 2005

Maruhom, M., Pagadian, Mindanao, Philippines, 5 July 2005

Matuan, M., Marawi State University, Philippines, 8 July 2005

McDonagh, S., Dalgan Park, Navan, Ireland, 21 June 2016

McHugh, K., Manila, Philippines, 9 July 2005

Minalang, L., Pagadian, Mindanao, Philippines, 5 July 2005

Mohamad, N., Marawi, Philippines, 8 July 2005

Nazareno, Y., Cagayan de Oro, Mindanao, Philippines, July 2005

O'Malley, D., Pagadian, Philippines, July 2005

O'Neill, P., Dalgan Park, Navan, Ireland, 20 January 2010 and Cagayan de Oro, Mindanao, Philippines, 9 July 2005

Quibranza, R., Cagayan de Oro, Mindanao, Philippines, 5 July 2005

Robinson, J., phone interview, 11 November 2009

Tabania, N., Mindanao, Philippines, 7 July 2005

Magazine Articles

Brannigan, J., 'Death of a Peacemaker', *Far East* (November 2001), pp. 10–11

Capalla, F., 'A Dialogue of Life and Faith', *Columban Mission* (October 1990), pp. 2–5

Colgan, J., 'Rebels Release Columban Missionary', *The Far East* (January/February 1998), pp. 6–9

Glynn, P., 'Life Goes on in Lanao', *Far East* (December 2001), pp. 4–5

Halley, R., 'A Magic Moment in Marawi', *Misyon* (November/December 2000), pp. 12–13

Hartford, D., 'Healing Wounds of History', *The Far East* (October 1996), pp. 15–17

Twohig, T., 'The Sultan and the Priest', *Columban Mission* (October 1990), pp. 27–8

Newspapers

Birmingham Evening Mail   *The Irish Times*
Irish Independent   *The Jakarta Post*

Manila Bulletin
Munster Express
People's Tonight
Philippines Today
Sunday Tribune
The Catholic Universe

The Manila Times
The Nation
The Philippine Star
The Philippine Daily Inquirer
The Washington Post
Waterford News and Star

Report

McKeating, C., 'Report on the Tragic Death of Rufus Halley' (unpublished, Manila, 2001)

Websites

Alan's Point – History and Contemporary Events: http://alan73.blogspot.com

Business World Online: www.bworldonline.com

Country Studies: http://countrystudies.us

Islamic Culture and Relations Organisation: http://cid.icro.ir

Newspapers.com by Ancestry: www.newspapers.com

Official Gazette: www.officialgazette.gov.ph

Philippines Government: www.gov.ph

Philippine Headline News Online: www.newsflash.org

Rappler: www.rappler.com

Reuters: https://uk.reuters.com

Stanford University: http://web.stanford.edu

The Catholic Bishops' Conference of the Philippines: http://cbcpwebsite.com

The Irish Times: www.irishtimes.com

The LawPhil Project: www.lawphil.net

The Vatican: www.vatican.va

The Washington Post: www.washingtonpost.com

Union of Catholic Asian News: www.udanews.com

US Office of the Historian, Bureau of Public Affairs: https://history.state.gov

ABOUT THE AUTHOR

© Laura Faherty

Jean Harrington co-founded Maverick House, a non-fiction publishing company, in 2002, where she remained as managing director until 2011. During that time she also set up an office in Bangkok and started selling and distributing books all around southeast Asia, as well as ghost-writing several books. Her first, *Survivor: Memoirs of a Prostitute*, sold over 20,000 copies. She joined the board of Publishing Ireland and subsequently became its president. In 2010 she was elected as the Irish representative to the Federation of European Publishers, where she remained until 2012, when she left publishing and started working in education.